'Meditate Like Mad'

THE ANTI-BRIDEZILLA BOOK

How To Calm The F**k Down And Still Manifest The Wedding Of Your Dreams!

By Madison Bound

© 2019 Madison Bound
All Rights Reserved

TABLE OF CONTENTS

Introduction 1
Foundation: Meditation Entry Methods 3
Meditation 1: BE WELL.. 6
Meditation 2: PERFECT FIT 12
Meditation 3: ALL THE TIME IN THE WORLD 15
Meditation 4: A FAIRY 'HAIRY' TALE 19
Meditation 5: WEATHER THE STORM......................... 23
Meditation 6: BALANCED BRIDE 29
Meditation 7: EVERYONE'S COMING 35
Meditation 8: DRESS SHIELD 38
Meditation 9: WORD PERFECT 41
Meditation 10: PHOTO-GENIC GENIE......................... 48
Meditation 11: MAKING A SCENE................................ 51
Meditation 12: BANISH THE BLUBBER....................... 54
Meditation 13: VENDOR MACHINE 59
Meditation 14: HEAT FOR COLD FEET 62
Meditation 15: WILT YOUR JILT TILT.......................... 69
Meditation 16: CENTRE OF ATTENTION 79
Meditation 17: FROM BRIDEZILLA TO BRIDE THRILLER 86
Meditation 18: OUT-OF-THIS-WORLD WEDDING 92
Meditation 19: SHE'S SO SERENE............................... 95
Meditation 20: PLANNING FOR JOY............................ 98
Meditation 21: HAPPY EVER AFTER 104
Author's Note... 104

INTRODUCTION

First, many congratulations -- you said, "Yes!"

You are engaged, and you've set a date.

What joy! How lucky you must have felt!

But then the planning began.

And the worries started to nag and pull at the edges of your mind.

Those shadowy little fears -- with their pesky prickly points -- get under your skin, jabbing you every time your attention moves to your impending marriage.

What if...

- ...we can't get the venue?
- ...we can't afford the wedding I want?
- ...I get sick on the day?
- ...I can't get the perfect dress I want?
- ...I can't fit into my dress on the day?
- ...my fiancé changes his mind and leaves me standing at the altar?
- ...I change my mind and just want to run away and stay single?
- ...the guests fall out / his mother is mean to me / his best man gives a stupid, upsetting speech?
- ...I just start crying and turn into a big blubbing mess?

- *...I do something embarrassing in front of everyone?*
- *... etc.*

(Etcetera, as in ALL the above, times a million other conflicted thoughts, fears, and worries!)

In this kooky guide for brides-to-be, you'll find plenty of ways to out-fox your fears, pacify your panic, and manifest the wedding of your dreams rather than of your nightmares!

Too often, we let our minds run riot and bully us into negative feelings and anxiety. With a major life event, like a wedding, this process can go off the scale. But you deserve a great wedding, so it's time to take control of your thoughts, your creativity and your destiny... using the power of creative meditation.

Are you ready to get started? Then let's begin.

Here comes the bride...

FOUNDATION:

MEDITATION ENTRY METHODS

For each of the heart-expanding mind-hacks in this book, you will be required to get into a meditative state first.

If you have never meditated before, here are four simple 'entry' methods you can choose from.

They will help you settle your mind and enter a relaxed state of mindful awareness...

Start by... Sitting cross-legged on the floor, back straight, head up as though the top of your head is comfortably suspended from a string tied to the ceiling. You may use a cushion to sit on if you wish. Or simply sit upright in a chair. Allow your hands to rest on your knees, palms up.

Close your eyes.

One – Progressive Relaxation

Beginning at the top of your head with your scalp – tighten the muscles, hold the tension, and then relax each of the muscles in your body, working systematically down from your head to your toes.

So, tighten and then relax your scalp, then your forehead and brow, then eyes, then mouth and jaw, neck and throat, shoulders/trapezius and upper back, chest, upper arms, forearms, hands and fingers, stomach and abdomen, mid and lower back, buttocks, inner thighs and thighs, hamstrings, knees, calves, ankles, and finally feet and toes.

Let your whole body relax, breathe calmly, and prepare to do your chosen meditation…

Two – Follow Your Breath

Tune into your breathing. Take four deep breaths, breathing in through your nose, filling your belly and chest, then blowing the air out through your mouth, completely emptying your lungs. Then allow your breathing to relax.

Breathe in and out through your nose.

Focus on the feeling of the air coming in and out through your nostrils. Count your breaths, counting on the out-breath. When you reach 10, start over again. Do this for a couple of minutes until you feel calm, then start your chosen meditation.

Three – Box Breathing

Breathe in for a silent count of four – "1 and 2 and 3 and 4" – then hold your breath and count to four. Exhale while counting to four in your mind. And hold the air out for a count of four as well.

Then repeat, breathing in for four, holding for four, exhaling for four, and waiting to breathe for four. Do this for a couple of minutes to get peaceful and ready to meditate.

Four – 100 to Zero Countdown

In your mind, slowly count down from 100 to 0 (zero) and imagine becoming calmer and calmer. This technique was popularised by the Silva Mind Method as an effective way to enter the relaxed 'alpha' brainwave state.

It's a good preparation for the meditations and visualization practices in this book for brides-to-be. You'll like it.

MEDITATION 1:

BE WELL

Every bride-to-be wants to look her best for her wedding, and you are no exception.

You want to have that 'glow' of happiness and well-being about you.

But, what if, come the big day:

... You've caught a cold?

... You've got the flu?

... You feel like spewing?

... You've got the runs?

... You're as bloated as a whale?

... You're breaking out in hives from all the stress?

...You're incapacitated or severely afflicted by a flare-up of any inherent long-term illness, condition, or disability that you may be living with?

In this meditation, we will prep your mind and body to manifest the best of health for your wedding day, and simultaneously be able to cope and adapt to any deviation from that ideal!

Use one of the four 'entry methods' to get quiet and peaceful; then take your pick from the following visualizations that will have you feeling fit-as-a-fiddle for your nuptials.

Empress Your Mind

The one place in life where you can truly rule as a mighty Queen is in the empire of your mind.

Here you are the Empress. You decide what to think. You decide what to feel. You decide whether to throw your power away by *reacting* to life or own your power by *responding* to life from a place of choice and wisdom.

Begin your meditation by imagining your golden throne raised up on a richly carpeted dais or platform. Create it in your mind's eye. Make it as beautiful, rich, opulent, and powerful-looking as you can.

Now, imagine stepping up on the dais, turning, and sitting upon your power seat, taking your rightful place as ruler of your world.

As soon as you sit upon your throne, you are enveloped by a sense of your enormous power. Energy surges within you, filling you with authority.

Whatever you say happens. Your instructions are always carried out. *Always.* A power you must use wisely.

So, use this power now to declare ...

"I love and approve of myself. I love and approve of my body. I love and take care of myself. I lovingly take care of my body. And my body lovingly responds with well-being."

Think ahead to your wedding day and declare with power and conviction:

"I WILL be fit and healthy on my wedding day. My body WILL feel better than ever. I WILL have an abundance of energy. I WILL have a tremendous sense of well-being. And everyone WILL see my radiant vitality and the joy sparkling in my eyes!"

Repeat this command daily, and any time any fearful thought of illness tries to sneak back into your mind.

(You can also make that same declaration in the present tense and experience the reality of it...*in the now!*)

Remember, make your statement as a command. You, the Empress, command it. It must be. Let your body lovingly serve you by complying with your wishes.

Dive into the Well of Being

Remember, the source of your health is within, so let us explore deeper inside, and discover the infinite repository of 'well-being' that exists within you.

Imagine that...

- There is a little wishing well located at the top of your head.

- Throw your attention, like a coin, into the well shaft.

- Follow it down the tubular shaft that runs through your body to an area two finger widths below your navel and two finger widths inside your body.

- This area, at the bottom of the well, is called the *tantien* or *dantian* in China and the *hara* in Japan. It is known as a Chi or Qi (life force) reservoir. Martial artists anchor their awareness to it and use this point as a source of balance and vital power. To get the feel for it, some visualize it like a pearl-sized vortex being held between the thumb and forefinger of a small hand.

- Imagine that your *tantien* is a portal into an enormous inner bank or 'fuel tank' located in your lower abdomen.

- Breathe in and imagine air flowing into the wishing well and traveling down the tube-like shaft to your tantien.

- Breathe out and imagine the breath flowing into that immense fuel tank in your belly.

- Repeat several times to get a feel for it. Then begin to imagine that the air you are breathing in (and out) is sparkling with vibrant golden light.

- This is the energy of universal vitality. The infinite all-powerful Life Force of creation itself.

- Breathe it in and imagine it filling up your vast inner fuel tank with its super intense energy and light. Imagine more and more of it pouring within you, filling up that fuel tank.

- Feel yourself becoming stronger, healthier, full of light, vitality, vigor, and energy.

- Imagine that this irrepressible energy fills the tank and then saturates through the fuel tank walls into the rest of your body, shining,

- healing, nourishing, rebuilding, and revitalizing wherever it goes.

- Imagine that whatever part of your body you put your attention on is immediately suffused with a huge surge of vital force. It's rejuvenating, life-giving and restorative powers fill you up and spill out of you in beams of glowing health and well-being!

- Soak in it. Bathe in it. Let your mind relax into it. Dip into this well of being and feeling supremely healthy whenever you need a boost.

- Anchor yourself to the tantien, and its feeling of vitality and energy, by holding your attention there. Charge it up daily, filling it with more and more vitality. Let it works its magic in your body to make you fitter, happier, and healthier all over!

Blooming with Health

The bloom of a bride's face is often remarked upon in romance novels. That inner glow of happiness and joy shines through in the luster of her cheeks. Being in love is one of the most healing feelings imaginable.

To develop your 'bloom'...

Imagine it's your wedding day and imagine that you are like a beautiful flower. A gorgeous fragrant pink rose. Pristine, sublime, and exquisite.

This is your day and, as the sun of attention and love shines on you with its warm, rich light, you open up and radiate your beauty.

Imagine that there is a giant, light-pink bud with its base just below the soles of your feet and its tip just above the crown of your head.

On your wedding day, this bud opens up to reveal its full splendid beauty. Imagine spirit or energy petals unfolding around you, so you are surrounded by these divine pink petals. Your aura is now a giant rose, and you are literally 'in the pink'.

Imagine, as you breathe in, that you can smell its sweet and blissful scent. Inhale that fragrance, again and again, letting its nectar-like perfume fill you up with happiness and euphoria. Allow yourself to soak in the glow of this rosy beauty and smile with all your being.

Imagine smaller but equally beautiful flowers opening at the crown of your head and in the center of your chest where your heart center is.

Let these radiate the fragrance of joy and abiding love upon the congregation and imagine everyone there being lifted up with a sense of peace, happiness, and joyous well-being!

Focus on LOVE daily, take good care of yourself, and use your three BE WELL meditations to revitalize your energy and you will be vibrantly healthy and glowing on your big day.

MEDITATION 2:

PERFECT FIT

Think of your wedding, and one of the first things to leap to mind is the all-important wedding dress. And the *'oh-my-god, are you going to fit in it on the day'* terrors that seem to strike every bride as soon as she's selected hers!

If you've been dogged by nightmarish visions of uncooperative zippers or seams bursting apart as you walk up the aisle, the following ideas will help you chill out and ensure you get hitched without a hitch... *or so much as a loose stitch!*

Get yourself into a meditative state using one of the four entry methods... and then:

Imagine the Absolute Worst... Okay, so no messing about with paltry concerns here, let's blow this worry up big time. Pretend it's your wedding day, and:

- Take your dress out of its protective cover and discover... it's as tiny as a doll's dress! *<shriek!>*

- Look in the mirror and noticed you've become a frickin' elephant! Literally, tree trunk limbs, giant big ears, and tusks.

    Or...

- You've got into your wedding dress, but suddenly half-way-up-the-aisle, you start turning into the Incredible Hulk. Your body starts sprouting massive muscles and, before you know it, your beautiful dress is a shredded mess of material through which all your bulging limbs and curvy bits are protruding!

- Or suppose you are just about to say your vows, when Holy-Moly-Moby-Dick you've turned into a massive blue whale! Your white dress is now just a patch of material on the vast bulk of your immense blubber-filled back. You give a great blast from your blow hole and wink lovingly at your tiny intended staring up at you in horror!

- Or suppose that there is a sudden violent gust of wind that blows your dress right off. ...*Good job you have on nice lingerie!*

- Or a plague of locusts swoops in and chews your dress all up before flying off, burping to the tune of the bridal march!

By taking your fears to the absolute extreme, multiplied by ten, you can laugh about them, right?

...*Right?!*

Okay, having maxed out the drama, let's tame that vision down a bit to...

Imagine an Unfortunate 'Situation'...

- The dress has developed a rip in transit – but your designated bride's maid sewing expert is on hand and applies some emergency repairs in double-quick time. Nobody will ever know.

- You go to put your dress on, but you can't get the zipper to close properly. But your sewing buddy can help you with pins, or by sewing you into it, or has a friendly local Wedding Dress Alterations Service on speed dial in case of last-minute mishaps. There are always workarounds if you keep your s**t together.

- Your dress is a complete no-go. It's so very disappointing, but the show must go on. You won't let anything stop you or ruin your day, and you have other beautiful dresses you can wear if needs must. Adapt. Improvise. Be cool. Chili Palmer cool!

Imagine the Most Fitting & Perfect Scenario:

- You've maintained your figure with regular exercise and ensured your food intake hasn't varied or increased during the stressful weeks of your wedding preparations. So, of course, when you go to put on your wedding dress, you slip into it easily and effortlessly, just as you did in the initial fittings, just as you did a week ago when you trialed it, and just as you did the day before when you slipped it on for a final check.

- Imagine yourself fitting into your dress perfectly, with the precision of a finely tooled engine in an expensive car or an exquisite but fragile piece of sculpture fitting into a protective mold for shipping.

- Feel the happiness and sense of satisfaction when you realize that the dress fits perfectly. Enjoy how good it feels on you. Hear the gushing compliments of your bridesmaids and relatives. Notice the approving glances of your guests and well-wishers when you appear. See the pride, pleasure, and love in your groom's face when he first sets eyes on you!

    You look gorgeous!

Meditation 3:

ALL THE TIME IN THE WORLD

So. Many. Things. To. Do. And. Organize! <Gasp!>

Whether your wedding is going to be low-key and intimate or huge and decadent, there are always so many tasks to tackle, arrangements to organize, and things to think about!

Sometimes it can feel like 'The Wedding' takes on a life of its own. One that swamps your life and takes away from your relationship with your fiancé.

Yes, planning a wedding can become a frantic and relentless occupation. There's a desperation to keep moving, keep tackling all the issues and concerns that arise and keep all the plates spinning to make it successful.

But great brides-to-be, like you, know that you need to take time-out to just STOP.

Stillness has enormous power in it.

It can reset your energy. It enables you to refocus and drop the unimportant.

In stillness, you regain perspective. Here, you can decide to let go of your anxiety, gain control, and make better decisions.

Use one of the four meditation starters to relax.

The Pause Button...

In this meditation, imagine just stopping mid-action in one of the many tasks of your wedding plan.

It doesn't matter whether you are imagining trying on wedding dresses for the first time, hashing out a registry list at a department store, checking out reception venues, auditioning DJs or bands, or chasing quotes from vendors and caterers – just STOP, right there, in the moment.

Imagine that everything stops when you do. The people around you are frozen mid-sentence. The bodies of your wedding planner, your mother, your BFF, or fellow shoppers are frozen in the midst of whatever action they were doing. The cars on the street outside are static; the birds in the sky stalled in mid-air.

Having pressed this imaginary PAUSE button, take the chance to look around and re-assess everything.

Scan Your Plan...

Imagine you can step out of yourself. Walk around within the various frozen scenarios that you think of.

This is free space, free time. Breathe easy.

You can go up to the various people there – including yourself -- to peer and prod at them. Look at them from all angles to really assess each person and where they are coming from.

Give yourself time.

Take a look at your own frozen body there. Notice any tension or stress in your face and posture. Smooth out your brow. Ease the tension from your lips. Massage the tightness from those shoulders.

Think how you would want to be in this scenario: Cool, calm, collected, happy and content, poised and in control.

If you are minded to, sprinkle some fairy dust, good luck, love or blessings over everyone present.

Dissolve the frowns and put a smile on every person's face. See things working out in your favor and everyone being happy with the choices and decisions made.

Then step back into your body.

When you are ready, you can imagine starting to move, and it will be like you pressed the PLAY button again.

Only now you are refreshed, you are relaxed, and you have those cool, calm, collected feelings you wanted.

Stop Still...

To practice this, day-to-day, just STOP at random moments wherever you are, whatever you are doing, and keep your body perfectly STILL for 5-to-60 seconds (save the longer sessions for when you are alone and/or not caught in a 'stress position' like balanced on one leg reaching up to a high shelf!).

You can randomize this STOP exercise by setting an alarm to go off on your watch or smartphone. When the alarm goes, you will just STOP wherever you are… (or at the next safest moment if crossing a busy street or running from an escaped tiger!).

As you do so, bring your awareness fully into the moment.

Notice everything. Really listen to all the sounds around you. Feel the sensations in your body, the movement, and temperature of the air against your cheek. Become totally calm and fully present in the moment.

...Then move on again!

While carrying out the many parts of your wedding plans, experiment with just stopping, bringing everything to an absolute halt for a moment or two (or thirty) of super-aware stillness.

Afterward you can continue you with your bridal, work, or life activities with a greater sense of control and time mastery.

Affirm often, and especially when you are doing the STOP exercise, that: "I have all the time in the world!" And you will.

(This STOP meditation exercise was prescribed by the fascinating and delightfully roguish Armenian mystic, G.I. Gurdjieff.)

MEDITATION 1:

A FAIRY 'HAIRY' TALE

Wind. Rain. Humidity. Junk food & alcohol binges. Innate ornery locks.

There are various causes of 'bad hair day' (BHD) but no bride wants to suffer from hilarious hair nor hideous hair on her wedding day!

After all, this is something you've been dreaming about your whole life (yes, even you, Miss Cool!).

You've seen more than enough Disney-dusted perfect weddings to know that every bride needs to have super glossy locks that can bounce, and swish, and hold their style to woo all who witness her passage up the aisle!

If the thought of a 'dodgy do' on the day is bringing you out in cold sweats, let's tackle that terror, tame the hair beast, and ensure the coiffure stays pure!

Doubtless, you will already be:

- Taking hair nutrient supplements in the months prior
- Securing the services of your favorite hairdresser
- Ensuring you have all your favorite and most successful hair products with you in ready supply

- Checking long-term weather forecasts
- Planning your route and transport from dressing room to wedding venue with as little exposure to the elements as possible
- There are many practical things you can do to finesse your follicles

Certainly, you will have all that in hand. But let's settle those BHD fears and get some spiritual help to make sure your beehive behaves, your bob is just the job, or your bangs are truly bangin'!

Get into a relaxed meditative state using one of the four meditation warm-up methods.

Meet Your Hairy Godmother

Now, we are going to create a little guardian angel whose sole mission in life will be to guard your hairdo on your wedding day.

This being will only appear to you, but they will be on hand to protect you from the BHD gremlins. It's an exciting responsibility and one they will take very seriously.

What form do you want your 'hairy godmother' to take?

It could be...

- A famous hair stylist (if you know of any)
- Your favorite local hairdresser
- A Disney-style fairy with magical powers
- Heck, it could be Adam Sandler as *Zohan,* the Israeli commando turned hummus-wielding,

crotch-thrusting hair-stylist from the comedy movie, 'You Don't Mess With The Zohan' …IF that floats your boat!

Bring YOUR chosen hairy godmother to mind, and make them, ooh, let's say about 3 inches (7.6cm) tall!

Let them appear in a clearing in your mind's eye.

Give them a wand…or, better yet, a magic-making comb and a BHD battering hairdryer!

Introduce yourself, make friends, and let your hairy godmother know your fears for your big day. Explain that you are deputizing her or him to protect your 'do' and make sure it is utterly splendid on the day.

Watch as they immediately put a magic charm spell on your hair. It spins a glossy glow all over it, like a force field of gloriousness that will repel dullness, lankness, and the dreaded frizz.

Imagine the roots of your hair immediately filling out and thickening with super strong keratin. It is bursting with vitality and health, which spreads right along each hair making your hair strong, glossy, and tangle-free!

Imagine that your magical hair guardian gives a flick of her comb. A stream of sparkles flies towards you, entering your third eye.

Immediately, you find your consciousness can leave your body.

Your point of awareness swoops out of your eyes, to the top of your head, where it shrinks down to be able to examine each hair microscopically.

With your hairy godmother in tow, you slide along the silky-smooth shaft of each hair, which now seems as wide as a road to you.

If you spot any imperfections or 'pot-holes' in the hair, your little magical hair guardian zaps it, and it is immediately repaired so that the satiny-perfection of the hair is restored.

Imagine that, in super-fast accelerated time, which is a blur of four seconds, you can cover your whole head, bringing every hair up to the highest standard, leaving each hair with a mirror-like gleam.

…

Check in with your hairy godmother whenever you feel a tinge of BHD fear regarding your wedding.

Listen as she/he tells you to "Relax honey! I've got this!"

Do what YOU need to do to get your hair looking great on the day, and rest assured that your hairy godmother will be backing you up all the way so that you look fabulous!

Meditation 5:

WEATHER THE STORM

Much as we'd all love to get married on a perfectly still, sunny and pleasantly warm day, the weather is a law unto itself.

If you are freaking out at the thought of gales flattening your marquee or blowing your mother-in-law's new hat away. Or of torrential rain putting the big dampener on your outdoor ceremony, giving you sea-weed hair, making a mess of your make-up, and turning your bridal train into a giant muddy floor mop, then let's see what mind-power can do to manifest the perfect day for you.

Sun Dance

Tribal peoples traditionally resorted to rain-making rituals to end severe droughts. Farmers prayed, too, for sunshine to end rainy seasons and dry out their crops for harvesting.

As a bride-in-waiting, you don't need to do a rain dance, like those of the Zuni Native Americans in New Mexico.

But a little ceremonial *sun dance* could help you manifest perfect weather for your wedding!

To symbolize sunshine, wear something yellow or gold to represent the golden rays of the sun.

Get out in nature. If it's private and near to your chosen venue, all the better. If the best you can do is the back yard or a park, that's fine. If it's the dead of winter, right now, and minus 20 degrees, make do with your imagination and stay warm inside!

Define a circle of about 6-to-9 feet or 2-to-3 meters. You can just pace this out or mark it out with some pebbles or bits of popping corn (to keep the golden yellow theme going).

Stand in your circle. Use yourfavorite method to attain a more meditative state. And place your attention on your wedding date. Think of the time and venues for the ceremony and reception.

Bring a smile to your lips as you imagine being there, looking up, and seeing a beautiful warm sun shining from a perfect azure blue sky.

Picture arriving at your venue and standing outside. Imagine closing your eyes for a moment, turning your face up towards the sun, and feeling its pleasant warmth on your eyelids and cheeks.

Breathe a sigh of relief and pleasure!

Now, in your circle, re-enact this moment. Raise your arms up and out wide, palms up, face up, and begin to just gently and calmly turn clockwise, giving yourself over to this sense of appreciation, gratitude, and enjoyment of the pleasant sun!

The sun is *smiling* upon you, upon your partner-to-be, and upon your family, friends, and guests.

Feel like you are beaming with happiness, shining with appreciation, and glowing with bliss! (Really get into it!)

Allow yourself to feel a deep sense of KNOWING that this is exactly how it will be on the day.

Cloud Disperser

In the video for Kate Bush's 1985 single, *Cloudbusting,* she and Donald Sutherland (playing psychologist and philosopher Wilhelm Reich) brew up a storm with their rain-making machine that creates clouds out of thin air!

But YOU can just as easily *disperse* clouds... using only the machinery of your mind!

Want to get some practice in?

...You know, just in case you need to clear some crafty cumulonimbus or nix some naughty nimbostratus that stray anywhere near the vicinity of your nuptials!

Here's how to do it...

- Get yourself outside on one of those days when there are little fluffy clouds scudding across the otherwise blue sky.
- Lie on your back (if you can) and get into a meditative, focused state.
- Pick one of the little clouds to focus your attention on.
- Gaze intently at it, while imagining it fading away into the blue. Think, "F**k off, cloud!"
- Keep staring at it and notice how the edges of it start to get thinner and wispier, and then the core of it will disperse too until eventually, it all goes away.

- You just disappeared a cloud!

Advanced practices:

- Make two small clouds join up
- Disappear a larger cloud
- Make a hole appear in a big cloud, so the sun shines down through it like a spotlight... *on you, you gorgeous little slightly-witchy superstar!*

"From a very early age, I found that I could influence the weather. If it was raining and I didn't want rain, all I had to do was imagine a clear shield covering the city to block the rain, and within a few minutes the rain would subside."

~ Alan Tutt, wedding photographer & author

Storm in a teacup

What if a storm is already brewing, threatening to disrupt and bring chaos to your wedding service?

Then it's time to roll up your metaphorical and metaphysical sleeves and beat that bothersome beast into submission.

There are four main types of thunderstorm, but with the following mad magical meditation, you can cap them all.

Use one of the four meditation warm-ups to get your mind tuned-in and turned-on, then put your focus on the approaching storm...

Now imagine one of those pretty bone-china teacups, you know, the ones you see fine ladies drinking from in period drama movies.

Does yours have flowery patterns on it?

As you think of the colors and pattern on your cup, imagine it growing bigger and bigger and bigger until it is this vast thing that fills the sky and hangs over the planet Earth like some immense UFO (but not, ahem, a flying *saucer!*).

Invert it, so that it's upside down, then imagine lowering it down over the approaching storm.

It's so huge that it easily covers and contains the entire storm. Slowly lower the cup to the ground, so that it traps the storm inside itself. Simultaneously make the cup smaller and smaller.

Imagine the storm shrinking too as the cup it is trapped beneath is returned to its normal size. You can imagine the tiny little storm buzzing like a trapped wasp beneath the upturned cup for a few moments.

With no inflow to sustain its power, the storm immediately dissipates. You can now imagine lifting the cup and seeing what remains disappear in a harmless little puff of vapor.

Have the feeling during this whole procedure of easily and effortlessly snuffing out the storm, just like you would snuff out a candle. Think of blanketing it, muffling it, closing it down, and turning it off.

With big hurricane-like storms, you can imagine reversing its spin to cancel it out (they move counterclockwise in the Northern hemisphere and clockwise when South of the equator).

Just imagine sticking a giant finger in it and whisking it the other way.

Or imagine pushing a giant stick into it, pouring in sugar, and making storm candyfloss which you can shrink down and feed to a goat or something!

Or imagine cupping it, as before, but visualize it spinning tighter and tighter, as it gets smaller and smaller until it becomes microscopic and finally, with a pop, completely disappears from this reality. To be released in some other unoccupied parallel universe …where it can help seed worlds with new life, for all you care, just as long as it stays the f**k away from YOUR celebrations!

Meditation 6:

BALANCED BRIDE

Falling 'head-over-heels' in love is wonderful but falling 'arse-over-tits' in your wedding gown is a big no-no!

If you are one of the many brides who gets upset thinking about the potential for a pratfall in the aisle, a face plant at the altar, or a grassy butt slide during the informal photographs, let's get you back on an even keel, sailing smoothly forward towards your life of married bliss!

Get ready for meditation via your favorite 'entry method'...

Hazard Detector

Imagine you have a built-in radar in your mind. It reaches out into your environment and scans for potential hazards.

It's a pretty good idea to have this working all the time, but if your fear of Calamity Jane moments is limited to your nuptials, it's fine to set it up just for that special occasion.

Imagine this hazard radar reaching out, scanning left to right and right to left, up and down, 360 degrees around you.

It assesses the floor and immediate surrounds for bumps, cracks, roots, puddles, slippery stuff, mess, sharp edges, corners, narrow parts, branches, handbags, stray feet, closing doors, and anything that your dress or shoes could get hooked on, snagged by, or caught up in.

It does this from your starting-out point, to and from your transport, and continues to do so when you reach and transit into your venue, if indoors, or along the route to and from the location of your outdoor ceremony and the same for your reception venue.

Imagine it flashing red in your mind's eye to alert you to obvious dangers, orange for things you should certainly take into consideration, and then green lights you when all appears to be clear and hazard-free ahead.

Take a moment to imagine that clearly working at YOUR wedding.

Your radar alerts you to obstructions, animals, naughty or clumsy children and big-footed flustered adults that might step on your train, bump, or trip you accidentally.

With awareness, you can safely navigate all these potential hazards before and after your wedding.

This outward operating radar will have the added benefit of helping you 'take-in' more of the experience of your big day, rather than being lost in your own thoughts and concerns!

Tightrope Walker

Imagine you are walking on a tightrope stretched across Niagara Falls or attached between two super city skyscrapers.

- The first time over you get to hold a balance bar. So, get out there on the wire and take one steady step after another. Feel the wire bend and swing under your weight. Feel a breeze tugging at your torso. Adjust your balance using the pole, keep your eyes focused ahead to the platform opposite, and keep walking. Take step after step until you reach the other side and step gratefully onto the platform and into your helpers' arms. Feel a sense of enormous relief and achievement! *You should be buzzing!*

- Having rested, you now have to walk back the other way – and this time it will be without the balance bar. Imagine doing that. Give yourself a serious wobble mid-way. And marvel at how you recover your balance, center your mind on your target – the platform on the other side – and carry on walking over the wire till you reach it!

- Repeat this visualization over and over, but each time add another challenge, like, i) carrying two glasses of water, ii) carrying a basket of restless kittens or puppies, iii) carrying two precious babies, iv) carrying a tray stacked with champagne glasses while wearing high heels; and vi) carrying your fiancé while dressed in your full wedding outfit and reciting your vows!

Pinned To The Earth

Philosophers and theologians may wonder, "How many angels can dance on the head of a pin?" but come your wedding day, only one angel will be dancing on a pin, and that's YOU!

Let me explain...

In this meditation exercise, you will anchor yourself to Mother Earth to make sure you are grounded, balanced, and thus less likely to fall and feel like a clutz!

Remember the *tantien* or *hara*?

That energy point located in your body a couple of inches below the belly button?

Martial artists use it as focus point to centre and 'ground' themselves – in other words, it helps them keep their balance and stay strong.

In Aikido, for example, they imagine the tantien (or 'one point') as becoming more and more concentrated, circling in on itself over and over, becoming smaller and smaller, until mind and body are unified at some infinitesimal point.

Martial artists can make themselves virtually immovable as though they are nailed to the floor, so that even many strong men cannot lift them. According to Koichi Tohei, author of 'Ki in Daily Life', they do this by:

- Keeping their attention at this one point
- Relaxing completely
- Letting their weight distribute naturally to the underside of their limbs and torso (as it does when you relax fully)
- Extending Ki/Qi/Chi energy

'Marital' artists, like you, can learn to achieve the same sense of balance, poise, and imperturbability!

Imagine there are concentric rings or circles extending out around you, like those you see on the surface on a smooth lake when you drop a pebble in it.

You can imagine these on a horizontal flat plane or on a vertical plane, but either way, imagine that these concentric energy rings surround your tantien at the very center.

These energy rings can be thought of as both rippling outwards to the edges of the Universe and concentrating themselves inwards from the Universe towards the one point in your abdomen.

Imagine that from the biggest, most furthest away ring, each ring within that gets progressively smaller and smaller until it shrinks down to become infinitely small and focused within the one point of your tantien.

Keep the image of Universal energy becoming evermore focused within that one point, that tiny needle prick of a point below your navel.

From that one point, extend your attention, your Ki/Qi/Chi energy straight down into the Earth, and imagine it sinking all the way to the core of the Earth like a solid steel needle pinning you to the Earth.

With your feet and legs (and butt, if you are sitting) extending with gravity onto the floor with the weight of your body going down through them, you can just imagine sinking that energy deeper and further down.

It goes down through your building, down through the soil, down through the substrate and the molten magma and into the solid inner core which is as hot as the surface of the sun and mostly made of an iron-nickel alloy!

When you take your 'trip down the aisle', keep your attention on this one point, keep great posture but relax your body, allowing your body weight to hang naturally to the underside, following gravity towards the center of the Earth, and imagine that you extend deeply from the one point to the core of Mother Earth.

She'll keep you steady as a rock and walking smoothly up the aisle with a serene smile of poise and control!

Meditation 7:

Everyone's Coming

"What if nobody shows?"

You've sent the invitations out, and hardly anyone has replied. Or perhaps you've had the RSVPs back, but you are scared people will forget, make last-minute excuses, not bother to show up, or be unable to attend due to some 'act of God' personal or natural disaster.

Making allowances for people's busy lives and following up with gentle reminders by phone, email, or text helps you cover the practical bases of getting clear on who has definitely accepted your invitation to celebrate your marriage with you, and making sure they remember to do so once they've accepted the invitation.

Providing detailed travel tips and venue directions will further ensure both guests and vendors can't go missing come the big day.

Beyond that here are some mad meditations to end your 'no-show' fears and give you peace of mind that your wedding will be well-supported.

Magnetic Marriage

Imagine that you and your intended are holding hands and together you are like a huge horseshoe magnet.

As a couple, you are the north and south poles of the magnet, the male and female, yang and yin. Your marriage union will be a special and magical event.

It's powerful magic when two people commit their lives to one another in love.

And that magic creates pure magnetism, an irresistible allure that pulls people to come and be a part of the joy.

Picture yourself and your groom, together at the altar, hand in hand, with magnetic rays splaying out into the world.

See all the people you have invited being drawn, like metal filings to a magnet, to come and celebrate the occasion with you. It's easy, natural, and works out perfectly for all!

(If it helps, imagine a translucent horseshoe magnet superimposed over the two of you, like an aura, and the magnetic rays radiating out to where they need to go. Imagine your invitees being captivated, mesmerized, enthralled by the invitation, and readily and joyfully accepting!).

Love's Lasso

Irish mystic Lorna Byrne claims everyone on Earth has their own personal guardian angel. Furthermore, the seer describes seeing thousands upon thousands of 'unemployed angels' that are just waiting to be given jobs and the opportunity to be of service.

YOU can be their employer!

Imagine calling upon these angels of love to be your cowboys and shepherds and fishermen tasked with the duty of rounding up all your guests and vendors to ensure your big day is a super success.

See 'God's gauchos' flying off to throw lassos of loving light over those guests who are being 'total cows' or 'stubborn asses' about replying to your invitation.

Picture your angels acting like spiritual Bo Peeps to round up your flock and bring them trotting safely to your venue door.

See them casting the net of love and capturing both the hearts and attention of all your invitees, and then drawing them inexorably to land at your wedding party!

MEDITATION 8:

DRESS SHIELD

"But what if my dress gets splashed, stained or ruined?"

With the white wedding dress representing the purity of love (or more rarely, these days, the bride's virginity), the thought of anything besmirching that pristine snowy purity strikes terror into most brides. What about YOU?

In this meditation, you will create an impenetrable force-field to act as a shield around your wedding dress. Coupled with your Hazard Detector Radar (Meditation 6), this can help keep red wine, gravy, mud, make-up, ink, blood, sauces, juice, chlorophyll, flower pollen, snot, and all other nasties at bay on your big day.

Get into a meditative state via your favorite starter method.

Engage Force Field

Take several slow deep breaths. As you breathe in imagine you are breathing in great energy from the Universe. Picture it as radiant, sparkling energy.

Imagine this energy streaming to you from the sun and the stars beyond. See it swooping down from the sky from all directions and coalescing into a mighty torrent that sweeps around you like a blazing, brilliant vortex of pristine, protective energy.

This energy encircles you. All nasties that dare to approach are flung off by its high-velocity rotations. Don't be surprised if your crabby, hyper-critical great aunt ends up in a tree.

If you microscope your vision down into that energy you can probably see rows of little boxing-gloved fists ready to bash, biff and knock-out anything that could ruin your big day!

Wield the Shield

E-textiles and smart clothing are already making inroads into the fashion industry as the future hurtles ever closer. But I want you to imagine your dress already contains advanced next-generation high tech.

Yes, you're going Star Trek for your trek up the aisle. And like Princess Leia (hopefully minus the cinnamon-bun hairstyle) you're going to declare Star Wars on the baddies and zap any evils that try to stain your outfit.

So, imagine that your wedding dress is -- like you -- not only beautiful but intelligent!

Like the SS Enterprise and the Millennium Falcon, it comes fitted with deflector shields. Any incoming missiles of mess that fly towards your dress are instantly zapped and repelled before they can reach it. Picture them popping and disappearing like flies getting zapped by an ultra-violet insect killer light!

A.I.s Up

Imagine further than your 'smart dress' is operated by the most sophisticated Artificial Intelligence computer system. It is programmed to protect. It permanently scans your immediate surrounds. Its data assessment systems calculate likely outcomes.

It can see when a sommelier has lost focus, or a waiter has raised stress levels, and are more likely to pour or serve unsteadily.

It knows when your 4-year-old nephew has snuck in a felt tip or been plundering his nostrils and escaped your soon-to-be sister-in-law's attention.

Watch as it deploys 'influence lasers' to change minds, create new thoughts, and deter those who might have clumsily caused harm to your dress.

The wine waiter 'wakes up' to his responsibilities and pours with extreme skill and care. The errant child veers off to visit with a favored grandparent instead.

Threats are swiftly and automatically averted!

Meditation 9:

Word Perfect

In Hollywood movies, the bride always says the right thing. She doesn't pepper her speech with annoying disfluency fillers like *ums* or *ers*. She speaks clearly and with feeling.

Whether it's exchanging vows or delivering a witty or romantic speech to her spouse at the reception, the Hollywood bride is always pitch perfect and on point.

But that's an actress with a script worked up by professional writers. She gets to do multiple 'takes' to get it perfect. In real life, you don't get that luxury. And, yes, it sucks!

If you're freaking out thinking you are going to mess up your vows or sound like a complete idiot in front of your fiancé's extended family, let's pull your mind out of that loop.

Let's lock into your innate loquaciousness so you are never at a loss for words. And unfurl your honey-tongued brilliance through some meditative mind-state shifts.

The Practice Room

Go into meditation and visualize a stage. In the spotlight on that stage is an altar or place where the exchange of vows can happen. You will 'go there' regularly to practice saying your vows.

Just imagine yourself standing there, in your wedding outfit, feeling full of love, happiness, and joy. That beautiful feeling makes you effortlessly confident and naturally expressive.

Rehearse your vows (or speech, if you intend to give one). Go over the scripts of your vows super slowly, feeling out every word. Notice how you can make slight changes in emphasis to adjust the intensity of feeling, the emotion conveyed, or the underlying meaning.

If you need to, you can chunk your vows into sections, to make them easier to remember.

Does your spouse have a long name that you are frightened of forgetting or getting muddled? Could you use some mnemonic device to help you remember them and in the right order?

Lady Diana famously got it wrong when she married Prince Charles. In front of a worldwide TV audience of millions, Diana called him *Philip Charles* Arthur George, rather than *Charles Philip* Arthur George. And look how that turned out!

Once you think you've got your vows (or speech) down pat, and you are happy with your delivery, start to sequentially include additional elements to the visualization, such as:

- Your fiancé and the wedding ceremony official
- Your bridesmaids, best man, and wedding guests
- The venue and any vendors or serving staff

If you can deliver your vows smoothly under those visualized conditions, the next step is to throw some curveballs into the mix.

See if you can stay calm, focused, and speak clearly and confidently when:

- Somebody in the audience farts loudly and repeatedly
- Everyone in the audience gets a fit of the giggles
- A couple in the groom's section *(ugh.. of course!)* start to argue loudly

If we 'up the craziness', could you carry on regardless even if:

- A workman sets to work with a jackhammer road drill off to your left
- A sudden swarm of wasps invades your venue, buzzing around you and your guests
- A full-scale *Bugsy Malone*-style cream-pie fight breaks out around you

Why not take it all the way? See if you can maintain your equipoise and continue to speak charismatically, while:

- WWI-style 'in-the-trenches' and 'on the frontline' explosions are taking place all around you. Imagine getting showered in dirt and debris, but managing to carry on effortlessly with your declaration of love!

Lip Service

If you fear dry-mouth and the inability to articulate in anything other than platitudes or grunts come your wedding day, the following techniques can help free your brain, unlock those lips, and turn you into a silver-tongued speaker.

Get into a meditative state and play the 'Association Game'. Randomly think of an item or thing. Let's say you chose a 'lemon'. Say out loud, "Lemon". Then just let the brakes off your mind and say the very next thing that comes to mind and then the next and then the next, firing them out one after another.

So, what might you associate with lemon? You might think juice, or rind, or squeezer, or tart, or something else completely. Let's say it's 'rind'. And then you immediately think, 'peel'. And that word in turns makes you think of the peal of bells, so you say, "Bell". Continue to force associations as smoothly and rapidly as you can for two or three minutes.

Once you've got the hang of that, change the rules, and play the 'Disassociation Game'. In this mental word game, you must think of a new word that is entirely unconnected with your starter word. Thus, if we were starting with 'cup', your brain might automatically run to saucer, coffee, tea, trophy, or bra, but they are all associated with the word cup, so they don't count. You need to stretch for a disassociated word instead. Like sand or bullet or whisker. And then push for a word unconnected to that one. Do this exercise for a few minutes, speaking out loud your chain of unconnected words, again trying to be as smooth and hesitation-free as possible.

Next up is the 'Stop, Drop, and Describe' Game. You can do this as an impromptu exercise as you go about your day. Imagine you are like an army scout on patrol in enemy country. When you come across enemy encampments or activity, you stop, drop down, and via your radio comms describe exactly what you see to your command. It's vital that you communicate clearly, accurately, and with as much depth of information as possible.

In your case, just pick the room you are in, the scene that surrounds you, or a view from a window and verbally describe the hell out of it.

(Little tip: Recording this can help reveal the flaws and gaps in your thinking and perception.)

Move next to Win Wenger's 'Image Streaming' practice. This is pure gold. Ideally, you will use a recording device for this. What you do is get into a relaxed, meditative state, then put your attention on the flow of thoughts, images, sounds, feelings, and sensations that flow constantly into your mind space.

Next, you begin to describe aloud, in the present tense, what it is you are perceiving in the stream of mental imagery. You must try to get a sense of and incorporate all the senses that are involved.

For example, as I close my eyes now, "I see a light cream screen backdrop slightly down to my right-hand side, and in front of that are two jaguar cats facing one another with golden orangey-yellow fur spotted with sable-black ring markings."

I want to include a description from my other senses in the image streaming process, so I listen (extend hearing imagination into the scene) and say, "I hear their deep throaty chug-chug purrs, and that deep sensuous vibration resonates pleasingly in my chest."

Reaching for more tactile detail (I extend mental hands into the picture) and say, "I run my fingers up through their thick fur feeling the warmth of their skin radiating through from underneath and feel a great sense of happiness."

Being a primarily visual thinker, scent, and taste don't leap to the forefront of my mind that often, that I am aware of. Therefore, once again, I must help the image stream process along by imagining sniffing whatever it is that I see in the image stream. That's to get a sense of its smell. Or I will extend a mental tongue in there to have a surreptitious lick and describe the imagined flavor!

Now, the idea of a 'stream' is that it *flows*. And the image stream mustn't be damned up too much by putting all these blocks in its way. This is all happening super quick. The primary thing is simply remembering to try to incorporate as many senses in your descriptions as possible while allowing the whole thing to flow and reveal itself to you.

As I close my eyes now, *"I am seeing rich, smooth, maroon-colored velvet leggings covering the bent knees of someone wearing an off-white soft woolen cardigan, while sitting in a wheelchair, which has thick black rubber wheels that bear pale light-grey scuff marks of wear. I am looking from an inverted position above the person, so they appear to me like they are upside down with the floor in the ceiling position. I can see the light reflecting off the shiny linoleum flooring of the nursing home or hospital passageway. There's a soft sweet, subtle scent of rose perfume, the undercurrent smell of floor cleaner, and along the hallway, where I can hear faint background sounds of pots clanging, the smell of gravy wafts in the lunchtime air...."*

Practice your spoken-aloud image streaming for at least 10 minutes at a time. Aim for fluency, smoothness, and multi-sensorial present-tense description. If you can record it, listen back to your image stream afterward. This helps create an important neural feedback loop that helps to enhance your inner and outer communication skills.

Get good enough at image streaming, and you should find you are never at a loss for words again, as you can rapidly associate or link to relevant things to say to keep the conversation going or to start a more meaningful dialogue.

Finally, we have the 'Just A Minute' game, based on the world-famous BBC radio comedy game show of the same name. In this game, you pick a random starting topic or subject, and you must speak about it for one minute without deviation, hesitation, or repetition of any words (other than the starting topic phrase).

Everyone thinks they will be good at this until they try it. Get a child to judge how well you do and prepare to be ruthlessly picked-up on!

(Room for a new hobby? Consider joining an improv class or group. It's a terrific way to force your mind to adapt to new scenarios so you can always think on your feet and act how you want to be perceived!)

Meditation 10:

Photo-Genic Genie

It may loom larger than life, right now, but someday your wedding will be just a memory.

Having great wedding day photos can keep those special memories fresh and rekindle the love from your big day.

You'll want to look back fondly at how fabulous you and your partner looked.

But what if something goes wrong on the day and you end up with crappy photos in which you don't look your best?

If you are one of the many brides-to-be that harbor this secret fear, use this meditation to ease your photo phobias...

The Camera Loves You

Imagine that your wedding photographer's camera is alive. It's sentient, and it's friendly.

You've seen plenty of movies with objects or machines that are conscious, so this shouldn't be hard to do. Think of Cogsworth the clock (from *Beauty and the Beast*), Bumblebee (from *Transformers*), WALL-E, or R2D2, for examples.

Expand this further and imagine that all cameras and phone cameras are alive and responsive to you.

Take a moment now to draw a feeling of love and affection into your heart. When you can feel it and feel that smile of warmth and pleasure come to your lips, radiate that loving feeling out towards the wedding photographer's camera, and towards all cameras that are ever pointed at you. *Yes, even security cameras!*

Just send all photo and video equipment a whole bunch of glowing, affectionate love. Include a healthy dose of gratitude and appreciation to those cameras too.

Think a blessing prayer towards them. Something like, *"Hi Camera, I want to say a huge thank you to you for taking wonderful images of me. You are such an amazing piece of technology, and I'm so grateful that you make me look so good in your pictures! Thank you, I like you, and I love you!"*

See your stream of love enter the camera, making it feel super happy.

You've made its day! No-one ever offers it any thanks! You've won it over and become its favorite person.

Dare I say it: *The Camera now loves you!*

Just Right Light

Keep your relaxed state and command your Photo-Genic Genie to appear in a puff of smoke!

Your Photo-Genic Genie is a photography wizard. A genius of lighting, posing and capturing the mystery and mood of the moment in captivating imagery.

If you can't physically touch it, give any camera you see before you a quick mental rub, and imagine that your Photo-Genic Genie will manifest in spirit to oversee things.

He or she will influence your photographer to get just the right angle, take advantage of the light perfectly, and capture the love you and your partner are feeling for one another so that it is manifest for all to see.

Don't be afraid to give Genie a wink and he or she will douse the whole setting in magic sparkles to transform the ordinary into the extraordinary and make your photos appear truly magical!

*(**More Eyes and Free Editing:** Why not invite your guests to take lots of impromptu and natural photos too – and to share the best with you after you return from honeymoon! Maybe you could offer a prize for the best pic to help them 'focus' better?!)*

Meditation 11:

Making a Scene

Unfortunately, every family tree has its share of miscreants, neer-do-wells, and reprobates. Hopefully, you pruned the more obvious prodigals and pariahs from your wedding invite list.

But there are always a few people that you cannot avoid inviting who will give you cause for worry.

Perhaps your fiancé's oldest sister is notorious for getting the devil inside her when she's had a drink or two?

Or your step-brother's threat to give a speech revealing your sordid college days is giving you middle-of-the-night panic attacks?

Let's immediately douse the flames on that fear wildfire and take your mind to a happier place.

Rather than worry about someone making a scene at your wedding, we'll invest that mental energy into setting the scene you want.

Scene-sational!

1. Relax into a meditative state using the 4-4-4-4 breathing method.

2. Use your mind to scan the guest list and identify possible 'threats' – the person or people who worry you most.

3. Take each person you are concerned about and imagine meeting with them. You can set up an informal coffee table in a pleasant space in your mind's eye.

4. Visualize the person arriving, and treat them with great affection and care, as you imagine sitting down for drinks with them.

5. Imagine telling them how pleased and grateful you are that THEY are coming to your wedding. Explain how you intend your wedding to be. Tell them exactly what the atmosphere will be like, so they know what to expect and what is expected of them.

6. Have them be very compliant and agreeable in your visualization, even if that is not how they seem in your real-life experience. Task them with the responsibility of helping to ensure that is how the wedding and reception is.

7. Ask them specifically to help you achieve it; say that you need their help, and you are relying on them to create a magical wedding experience for you and your fiancé, and for everyone present. Have them willingly accept the challenge.

8. If there are specific things that worry you about this person, take steps in your visualization to counter that threat. Have the bad drunk behave with sobriety, moderation and respect. See your often tactless friend behaving herself impeccably.

9. Does your mother appear to detest your mother-in-law? Do you worry your wasp-tongued snobbish aunt will give loud voice to

her opinion that the groom's family are rude and uncouth? Whatever causes you fear, aim a giant mental vacuum cleaner at it, turn it on full force, and see it sucking all the poisons and toxic vibes out of your guests, leaving them clear, calm, happy and loving.

10. Whenever a picture of your wedding or reception guests come to mind, give it a quick mental spray of polish. Then wipe it over so that all the grime and worry is removed, and it's left bright and shiny!

11. Paint the picture of how you want your wedding to be. Set the scene you want. See it unfolding with everyone getting along, having fun, and being loving and joyous together. Make THAT the intention, and that's exactly how it will turn out.

Meditation 12:

Banish the Blubber

OMG! You are getting *married.* That's HUGE!

But consider all the pressures of preparing for the event. Then of the focus switching totally to you and your partner on the day. How you will be declaring your love for one another.

You've waited your whole life for this. It's going to be romantic, emotionally intense, and deeply impactful.

And the nagging question is…

Are you going to be able to handle it? Or is there a strong risk you will end up dissolving into floods of tears?

Nobody wants to be that blurry-eyed blubbing bride!

No girl wants mascara running down her face, snot bubbles blooming from her nostrils, nor to freak the hell out of her beloved with her emotional breakdown!

You need to find the inner space where you can be serene, loving, and calm while enjoying the full richness of the experience of your love match.

Having a Ball, NOT a Bawl!

Get into a meditative state and imagine it's your wedding day. Your mission for this day is giving and feeling love and enjoyment.

How much love can you handle? How much joy are you willing to experience? Some people are easily overwhelmed by love. They have a low threshold for joy. And one way they cope is by crying.

By activating their lacrimal glands *(that's 'tear ducts' to you and...eye!)*, they unconsciously attempt to balance out their strong positive emotions. Creating some negative emotion (tears) helps them to restore a sense of emotional balance and calm.

Being a happy crier, shedding tears of joy, being deeply moved by meaningful events... On the face of it (but not your wedding day face), that all seems like a good thing. Clearly you have empathy and a rich emotional intelligence that helps you relate to your fellow humans.

You enjoy the full gamut of the emotional experience. But on your wedding day, you want to look and feel your best, not end up a soggy, sobbing mess.

Introducing...

The Tearminator

Imagine a robot you from the future, built long after you are married, who travels back in time, to zap your lacrimal system and prevent any on-the-day waterworks.

This robot, powered by a super advanced A.I., looks like you, but it's a you that has been blended with Arnold Schwarzenegger, complete with Austrian accent and corny one-liners!

...*Lovely!*

In a storm of time-travel lightning, imagine this Tearminator drops naked to Earth in present time. All glistening muscles and boobs.

Your badass robot-self beats up some bikers, takes some boots, jeans, shirt, leather jacket, sunglasses, and a motorbike and roars across town to your place.

It has one mission. It's not to kill Sarah Connors, but to chill YOUR over-active emotional system!

Imagine the Tearminator, aiming her ray gun at you, firing a laser deep into your limbic system.

Behind her robotic eyes, her HUD (heads-up display) read-out is monitoring your hypothalamus and its hard-wired interaction with your autonomic nervous system.

Part of the HUD shows numerical figures for the quantity of acetylcholine (a neurotransmitter that controls and stimulates tear production) being produced now and that can be produced in the future under different scenarios.

Imagine that the laser ray contains a software update that instantly reprograms your limbic system.

It is date specific, set to your wedding day, and now gives you a complete free pass to be serene and calm on that day.

Good Judgement Day

You will get to experience great love, but you will have the presence of mind to enjoy it in balance and grace without tripping out into emotional extremes.

The acetylcholine production will suffice to keep your eyes shining, beautiful, and healthy, without going over the top into Blubbsville!

Now picture yourself getting married and enjoying your reception festivities.

Imagine the various scenarios along the wedding day path that previously might have triggered your tears.

Perhaps during the lead-up. The interaction with your parents or friends and their emotions for you. Maybe the sight of all your guests waiting expectantly at the wedding venue would move you deeply and making it suddenly all seem so real.

Perhaps the excitement of your bridesmaids or the cuteness of your ring-bearers could be a hot button. What about your dad or step-father giving you away?

Then there's your groom, standing there waiting for you, nervous, excited, adoring, looking so handsome in his wedding suit, and so clearly wowed by how wonderful you look.

No Problemo

The new reprogrammed you can just smile gratefully into every part of the whole experience. Notice how you feel an inner vastness. A sense of great space to allow all this simply to be.

You now have the feeling of deserving these blessings and of being completely okay with feeling so much beauty, pleasure, and poignancy.

Having visualized yourself handling all stages of the wedding with emotional serenity and grace, you can end the meditation by saying, *"Hasta la vista, cry baby!"*

MEDITATION 13:

VENDOR MACHINE

A wedding is a huge event – not just for the bride and groom but for all their families and guests as well. There are a lot of people to keep happy, and much of that will be contingent on the presence and efficiency of your wedding vendors, suppliers, and service personnel.

No wonder many a bride-to-be ends up sweating bullets over whether her suppliers will show up AND deliver to the standard she expects.

There are countless apocryphal horror stories out there of caterers going AWOL, leaving banquets dependent on hastily arranged pizza deliveries, or of bands getting arrested so that receptions are left with no music to dance to.

You don't want THAT!

Go Pro

Hire professional wedding vendors who work to contract. While the thought of saving money by hiring a talented amateur DJ or hobbyist photographer can be appealing, you'll regret it if they turn up late, drunk, or in sweat pants, or just don't arrive at all!

Keep In Touch

Make regular email contact with your vendors prior to your event. Phone to confirm everything is on-track in the days immediately prior and confirm arrival times.

Details & Dates

Supply each vendor with detailed information regarding your wedding and reception itineraries and schedules. Include travel/traffic considerations, how to get to your accommodation, wedding and reception venues, and where they can park.

Tips

Are gratuities expected for your service personnel? Prep your cash envelopes in advance. Delegate a trustworthy (non-drinking) relative to hold the cash and to dispense it to the correct people after the event has gone smoothly.

Besides taking practical measures like those above, you can dispel your vendor fears using the following meditation…

Make It Push-Button Easy on Yourself

1. Use one of the four intro methods to enter meditation.

2. Now imagine a giant vending machine (the size of a building) that is designed purely for brides-to-be. It is a super high tech and totally efficient 'Wedding Vendor' Vending Machine!

3. Imagine that you have a large, heavy gold coin in your right hand. This isn't Bitcoin, baby; this is a Bridecoin!

> **Notice:** On one side of the Bridecoin, there's a picture of you smiling. On the other, it says 'WEDDED BLISS.'

4. Around the rim of the coin, you can read the phrase, 'The bearer is entitled to get happily married.'

12. Put the Bridecoin in the slot of the wedding vendor vending machine. Look over the menu, then start pressing buttons to place your order for the various vendors and suppliers whose services you need to engage.

13. From hairdressers and beauticians to wedding officiants, wedding planners, caterers, transport providers, florists, photographers, videographers, bands/DJs, and bakers. Put in your order!

14. Hear the vending machine whirr and hum into action. Picture the various cogs and wheels turning efficiently within its production engine.

15. Imagine this vending machine operates like a giant 3D-bioprinter. You press the button for a specific type of vendor. Seconds later it has printed out a perfect, top-of-the-line, utterly reliable vendor who is delivered out of the front of the vending machine and straight to the required time and place you will need them.

16. Revel in the perfect machine-like efficiency of the whole process. Constantly see and picture all your vendors and suppliers not only meeting but exceeding your wedding expectations. For you, they are timely, efficient, and a pleasure to work with.

17. Continually visualize everything working like clockwork on your big day!

MEDITATION 14:

HEAT FOR COLD FEET

Uh-oh, are you having second thoughts?

Is your mind fretting over whether you are making the right decision? Do you fear a loss of independence? Are you feeling a tad scared of being trapped in a relationship with just one man for the rest of your life?

It's normal to have a few doubts – especially if you start to feel overwhelmed by your wedding planning. But don't mindlessly fan the flames of those fears and let them turn into a wildfire of trepidation!

You need to get calm and get your runaway skepticism under control again. The monkey mind loves to create mischief with all of its 'What ifs'.

> What if he's not my soul mate? What if we run out of things to talk about? What if it doesn't work out? What if there is someone better out there?

...You know how it rumbles on and on!

If your feet are metaphorically 'cold', it's most likely because your mind/brain is so overactive it's hogging all the blood flow!

Find your inner peace, where gratitude and love abound, and you'll probably feel a warmth suffuse your whole being... from head to toe!

But before we attempt to turn up the heat, let's get to a place of clarity, so we can examine your fears honestly and see whether they have any basis in reality.

Taking The Temperature

In this meditation, we are going to explore the range of temperature you can experience in your relationship. Especially with regards to your thoughts about getting married and becoming a wife. Let's start by…

Feeling An Icy Clarity

Click your fingers and imagine you are instantly transported to the South Pole. You're lucky; it's one of those rare moments when there are no storms blowing. Instead, it's a perfectly still calm day. But all around you is snow and ice stretching to the far horizons. Even the sky looks white and crystalline with absolute coldness.

The scenario is:

- You are sitting on a rock beside a small pool of blue glacial water with lumps of ice floating in it.
- Imagine removing your snow boots and your thick socks, and then plunging your feet in the glacial water.
- *OMG! It's f-f-f-f-freezing!*
- Notice that:
- You are thousands of miles away from your fiancé, your families, and all the wedding plans.

- You are completely alone in this desolate but peaceful landscape. You can see in all directions.

- A sense of total clarity comes over you in this place.

From your stillness and peace, examine each of your fears, one by one, and ask:

- Is this a genuine fear or just a mind fart (attention-grabbing hot air)?

- Is this fear specific to my relationship with my fiancé or is it part of a pattern of fear that I have experience in other areas of my life too?

- What evidence do I have to support this fear? What evidence contradicts this fear?

- Are there better ways of looking at this?

Use the peace and icy clarity of meditation to be honest. Be honest about how your mind works. Be honest about how you are feeling. Be honest about the roots of your doubts.

Be honest about your understanding of the sacrifices you'll make in giving up your single life and the compensatory benefits that marriage can bestow upon you in exchange.

Give your intuition time to speak:

- Listen to your body.

- Welcome your fears and any negative feelings as best you can without trying to suppress them.

- Give them space to be acknowledged and then let go of if they are not serving you.

Feel the Cold

Focus on the coldness of your feet in that icy water. Imagine if you were left there in Antarctica forever. Alone. Cold. So very cold.

Imagine if you never got to see your fiancé ever again. Never got to see his smile. The sparkle in his eyes. Never got to feel his hands on your waist, nor the press of his lips on yours.

Imagine how you'd feel if you never got to hear his voice whispering his love for you in the middle of the night. Never again heard his warm laughter as you fool about and tease one another or cuddle up on the couch together. Never again got to feel the magic of making love together…

How would THAT be?

If, having examined your relationship in the cold light of (a South Pole) day, you recognize that you do want to go ahead, that your fears are groundless and just the tittle-tattle of a worrying mind, then I've just one thing to say:

"Let's warm your relationship tootsies and get you married, girlfriend!"

Tropical Toes and Hot Sole Mates

In meditation, click your fingers again, but this time imagine yourself sitting on a beach in a warm tropical location watching a glorious sunset with your fiancé. You have the beach all to yourselves making this a private space for you both to enjoy one another.

The sand is still warm from the day as you push your toes and feet into it.

Just in front of you, your man has dug a fire pit, and lit a beautiful fire of driftwood.

Remember some of those doubts you used to have back at the South Pole? Imagine throwing them in the flames and watching them burn to nothing!

Feel the thaw...

With a big smile, stretch your legs out towards the crackling flames and wiggle your toes as you feel the radiating heat warming and caressing the soles of your feet.

Life is good. Feel it. Celebrate it. Be grateful for it.

You're in love with life, in love with love, and in love with your man!

<Turn up the intensity dial on those loving feelings.>

Imagine leaning in towards your beloved and sharing a passionate kiss which sends tingles of pleasure throughout your body.

Take a deep breath, noticing the salty scent of the sea, the fragrant wood smoke, and the background scents of tropical flowers.

Look at the orange flames, and the orangey-pink sunset beyond, and feel the flames of your love within you.

Imagine inhaling the warm colors of the sun and of the flames and of your pleasure deep within yourself.

Feel that warm glowing light being drawn in on your breath down to your heart center, where it mixes with the inner sunshine of your love and your joy.

Imagine that warm glow radiating throughout your body. Picture and feel it filling every part of you with light, warmth, and comforting feelings of safety from top to toe.

Keep breathing in that light and filling yourself with that warm loving feeling. In your mind, hear yourself saying "Mmmmmm" with the sensual pleasure of it.

Notice how eventually that warm light starts to spill out of your skin, flowing out in radiant beams of love, until every part of you is shining, beaming, radiating out this warm pink-orange light of warmth, affection, and love!

- ✓ Feel love for yourself and radiate that love to yourself.
- ✓ Feel love for your man and radiate your love to him.
- ✓ Feel love for your decision to marry and share the adventure of life together. Project that love forth to your marriage and to your future married life.

Cocktail Hour

Sex on the beach, anyone?

As an optional 'happy finish' to your meditation, imagine making love with your partner there on your sunset-lit tropical beach. See yourselves surrounded by a flaming, heart-shaped halo of that pink sunset light. With your feet being warmed by the fire, be sure to fantasize having orgasm after orgasm!

(Pull Your Socks Up! A 2005 Dutch study suggested that women find it 30% easier to orgasm when they wear socks in bed. Not only does it improve blood circulation, it further enhances the feeling of comfort, safety, and security that a woman needs to let go and enjoy herself fully. To remain focused on the pleasure of your wedding, keep those feet warm so you can let go and enjoy the experience!)

Meditation 15:

WILT YOUR JILT TILT

"Never mind MY cold feet, what if my fiancé chickens out and leaves ME standing at the altar?!"

With a massive 20% of weddings called off ahead of time, it's not surprising if you've been secretly suffering 'jilt-tilt' at the thought of being abandoned at the last minute by your man.

Nobody wants to be left in the lurch at the front of a church!

You want to feel 'pumped' on your big day, not dumped!

Getting jilted is the ultimate humiliation for any bride-to-be (lots of grooms get jilted too), as you are left to face your guests and confess that you've been thrown over and deserted…

Let's ensure that can't happen to YOU!

Weighing His Heart

Ancient Egyptians believed that when they died, Maat, the goddess of harmony, truth, and justice, performed a weighing of the heart ceremony to decide whether the spirit of the person qualified to travel into a heavenly afterlife.

The heart had to be lighter than an Ostrich feather; something that was achieved by the person doing many good deeds during their lifetime.

You must weigh the heart of your fiancé to determine whether he is truly worthy to move forward and live with a heavenly and happily-ever-after wife!

Get into a relaxed meditative state and imagine yourself as the goddess of your upcoming wedding. Because, of course, you are!

In a way, a wedding is the 'death' of the single life. Many men (and women) secretly dread the ending of their singledom and its perceived freedom to pursue their selfish desires as and when they please.

They fear losing something, rather than focusing on the end of loneliness and the opportunity to be reborn into and gain a new life of intimate relationship, deep love, and life-long companionship.

Many people have grown up without growing up at all. There are lots of 'adult children' out there who have been indulged their whole lives.

Society has changed. Many young people have never really had to share, learn to be generous, or learn to do things for others out of kindness, a sense of responsibility, or simple respect for others.

Imagine that you are sitting on a throne of justice in your golden palace.

Before you, the scales of truth hold a white ostrich feather on one side and the heart of your beloved on the other.

As the goddess of truth, ask yourself:

...Is my fiancé a man or a boy?

...Is he responsible or irresponsible?

…Does he embrace commitment in other areas of his life or run from it?

…Is his heart light with goodness or heavy with selfishness?

…Is he capable of wounding me by letting his fear override his professed love for me?

…Is he true to me alone?

…Does he have honor?

Examine and assess from the greatest clarity and honesty you can find within yourself.

Trust your intuition and observe which way the balance of the scales of truth shifts.

If his heart if light and good, the side of the scales with the feather on it will dip down because it is heavier than his heart.

If his heart is heavier than the feather, you may need to do some soul searching, and have some deeper discussions with him.

Find out where you both really are. Does he feel inspired to marry you rather than compelled?

Do you need to challenge him to prove just how much he loves you and that he is truly committed to spending the rest of his life with you?

Be open with one another and examine your deeper fears about marriage. Get a clearer sense of where he is. Bringing fears out in the open can stop them from festering and ballooning into irrationality. In the clear light of day, you can see your fears for what they are and develop workarounds and solutions.

Refocus on the joy of marriage, this wonderful opportunity to commit to each other and promise oneself to the other! Talk it up so you are both as excited about it as on the day of the proposal.

Otherwise, why get married at all if you are not both 100% committed to the idea?

Brave Hearts

Courage has is origins in the Latin word for heart: cor. In this meditation, imagine your man displaying great acts of courage and feats of bravery. See him as a man with a big heart.

Take the plots of action movies and adventure books, or real life tales of heroism from history, and insert your fiancé as the heroic main character.

Otherwise, simply invent your own scenarios where bravery and courage are called upon.

Visualize your guy:

- Rescuing a kitten from high up a tree in a storm
- Walking a tightrope across Niagara Falls
- Standing up to a bully who is persecuting someone
- Staying true to his beliefs even in the face of persecution, mockery, or violence (like Jesus or Rosa Parks)
- Distracting a vicious bear or lion, giving you time to get to safety

- Giving a speech to a hostile audience about a cause he passionately believes in and winning their respect

- Persisting stoically and without complaint through some kind of physical ordeal or survival challenge

- Demonstrating total loyalty to you, his family, or his friends when faced with immense pressure or temptation to do otherwise

There are all kinds of ways that a person can show courage and bravery... from the small acts of courage necessary to endure illness, disability, difficult circumstances or challenging environments to the grander heroics typified by military, police, emergency, fire and rescue personnel.

Keep visualizing your guy triumphing over adversity. Pressing forward through difficulty. Setting fear aside to focus on doing what needs to be done – because it is the right thing to do.

Every man wants to be heroic, to be seen as brave and courageous. Find little ways to compliment your boyfriend on his courage, bravery and daring, his willingness to try new things with you and the ways he challenges himself to grow as a person.

Take any opportunity to tell him how you admire him for stepping up, taking responsibility, and being a man.

If you frequently praise him (and reward him with your affection) for these positive qualities, you'll be 'priming' his mind to want to live up to those ideals even more.

In a similar way, speak often and positively of life beyond the wedding and all the things you are looking forward to doing and creating together. Make sure your wedding can always be seen as a gateway to a better, happier life together not as some monstrous ordeal.

Chains of Love

In this mini-meditation, you are going to work up a sweat at the forge of destiny, making the links and the ties that bind two people together.

"Love binds everything together in perfect harmony."

~ Colossians 3.14

If the love between you and your partner is weak, many things could cause it to break.

In cases where brides have been jilted, their grooms have offered excuses like:

- "I finally realized she was too controlling."
- "I wasn't ready to let go of adventure."
- "I panicked because my tux didn't come back from the cleaners."
- "Leading up to the wedding, I kept dreading the future rather than being excited about it."

While brides who jilted their fiancé have said things like:

- "I just couldn't see myself being with one person for the rest of my life."
- "My maid of honor confessed her love for me, and we ran away together."

- "I got a stomach bug and was on the toilet the whole time!"
- "It doesn't matter, turns out he was sleeping with my step-mother!"
- "I got my revenge for all the times he cheated on me!"

How strong are the bonds you and your fiancé share?

You can build and strengthen the psychic love-ties that first drew you together and made you want to get married.

Here's how…

1. Get into a meditative state.
2. Breathe down into your heart center in the middle of your chest. This is the gateway to an infinite ocean of love that exists within your being.
3. Think of the one you love. Smile into that feeling. Breathe into it and let it expand as a pleasurable warmth in your chest and feeling nature. Soak into that nice smiley loving feeling. Enjoy it. Relish it. Let it grow.
4. Continue to breathe in and out, fanning the flames of that love, letting the feeling grow and grow.

    You can imagine breathing love in from the Universe (or from God, if you are that way inclined) and breathing out love to the Universe – to your lover, to your family and friends and acquaintances, to your pets, plants, home and possessions, to the people and living creatures in your town or city, in your country, and on your planet.

5. Imagine your partner sitting knees to knees directly in front of you, also meditating. As you breathe in, they breathe out, as they breathe out, you breathe in. You breathe out and radiate loving light towards them. They inhale that loving light. When they breathe out, radiating even brighter warmer loving light to you, you simultaneously inhale that love. Continue for a minute or two.

6. Now visualize this loving light growing ever stronger and more intense, and billowing all around you. Watch as it weaves back and forth, and around and around you both, forming a cocoon of purest love that envelops you and your partner together.

7. Imagine holding your hands out, supplicant style, with palms showing. Your fiancé does the same. Picture radiant aura-like strings of hearts bursting forth from each of your palms, streaming across to your beloved. Strings of hearts are also bursting forth from your man's palms too. The hearts link up and merge, yours with his. More chains of hearts encircle you both in their joyous protective and blessing energy.

8. Crank up the dial on the intensity of love. Let it shudder through you. Let it overtake you in its all-consuming bliss. Give yourself up to this creative act of benediction. This is where you forge the deepest links of Love.

9. Imagine gazing into one another's eyes. And loving light pouring back and forth on your sight lines.

Your gaze directs your love deep into his eyes, deep down into his soul, deep into that space where you are totally One. His look of love is equally penetrating, his love pouring into your eyes, deep down inside you to the core of your being, beyond the ego, beyond the illusion, to where you and he are completely unified, One and the same.

Know yourselves to be forever joined.

There are more extreme versions of this meditation. Some seek to tie their partners down, to imprison them with heavy chains of metal not just love. And they might be tempted to visualize such chains linking one to the other or being encased in the encircling golden band of a giant wedding ring. In English slang, spouses are jokingly referred to as 'the old ball and chain' and some fearful brides have even imagined such things imposed upon their grooms to anchor them to the spot. Ultimately the metaphor of ownership, slavery, or restriction is not a good one for a happy marriage.

Bryan Ferry sang about being a slave to love. We can all resonate to the addictive quality of romantic love and lust. But it's better to enslave yourself to love. Meaning dedicate yourself to being a loving person, to choosing love and kindness as your modus operandi with your chosen partner and with everyone else.

Love is a multi-directional emotion; when you feel it for others you can simultaneously feel it and enjoy it for yourself.

And when you feel it from others, you can simultaneously let your happiness and sense of love shine out to bless others too.

The sun shines in all directions and upon all. As does love.

"Let there be spaces in your togetherness. And let the winds of the heavens dance between you. Love one another but make not a bond of love: Let it rather be a moving sea between the shores of your souls."

~ Khalil Gibran, The Prophet

MEDITATION 16:

CENTRE OF ATTENTION

Some people crave attention. They'll happily seize the mic and hog the limelight. Being center stage is their paradise.

But around 75% of people experience stage fright and claim to fear public speaking more than they fear death!

That means three out of every four brides are likely to have some trepidations over their upcoming wedding.

Social phobia and speech anxiety operates across a sliding scale of severity.

At one extreme it can manifest as crippling dread that can make the sufferer vomit, suffer panic attacks, or physically run away!

On the milder end of the spectrum, the person will experience butterflies in their stomach and a lack of sleep the night before but knows that they can survive the experience even if it's not much fun for them.

What about you? Where do you fall on the spectrum?

How do you feel about saying your vows in front of all those people?

What comes up when you think of everyone looking at you on your wedding day?

Hopefully, you are looking forward to being the Star of the Day. If so, great.

But if just thinking about getting married in front of a crowd is triggering your gag reflex... *you might want to seek professional help from a psychiatrist or get some hypnotherapy sessions to lessen your phobia!*

For those with less severe levels of SAD (social anxiety disorder), scopophobia (fear of being stared at), glossophobia (fear of public speaking), or enochlophobia (fear of crowds), the following meditations can help dispel your anxiety and enable you to enjoy your big day.

Address Rehearsal

One classic way to blitz your fears of standing up and speaking in front of your congregation of guests is *practice.* You can't physically practice getting married, over and over, but you can rehearse it mentally hundreds of times. And imagine yourself loving everything about it each time.

Before you begin, you need a process to eliminate your fear thoughts and replace them with happiness, confidence, and elation instead.

For mild fears, one effective 'mind-tool' you can use is the NLP Swish Pattern.

To use it, imagine a scene from your wedding. Perhaps it's walking up the aisle with all the guests turning to look at you. Or the moment when it is your turn to declare your vows in front of everybody.

Play it through once completely in your mind. Maybe you tend to imagine feeling some nerves as everyone stares your way or you imagine stuttering over your vows.

As soon as you notice anything negative, like that, imagine a new, improved version blasting onto your mind screen while imagining that old version shrinking away into the far distance and disappearing.

The new mental movie should be brighter, more colorful, and richer in every way – and, in this new version, you imagine smiling happily at all of your guests as they turn to admire you and/or speaking confidently and lovingly as you effortlessly deliver your vows.

The key is to 'swish' a new, improved mental movie of your wedding into place instantly and whenever you notice a moment of doubt, fear, or trepidation about any part of your wedding and reception activities.

Previously you might have had a trigger thought like, "Oh no, everyone will be looking at me and judging me!" or "I bet I screw up my vows!". That would trigger corresponding negative emotions while you'd play your 'disaster movie' in your imagination.

Now, you will instead immediately blitz those negative trigger thoughts out of your mind, by blasting the new, improved movie over the top and shrinking the old worry movie out of existence. Do this repeatedly until it becomes automatic!

What if your fears are stronger and more... *phobic?*

Back From The Future

Imagine you are comfortably seated in a movie theatre. You are about to watch a movie about your wedding. *You'll love it -- it has a happy ending!*

Now imagine that you step out of yourself to one side, so that you are now watching yourself about to watch yourself getting married on the big screen.

Imagine the movie starts. It starts at a point before the wedding when you feel safe and it will end at a point after the wedding or reception when you again feel safe.

You watch yourself, seated there, watching the screen as your wedding and reception (including all the 'scary bits') play through on the screen. You can't see the movie you just see yourself watching it. The movie comes to an end after the wedding, and/or reception has finished.

Imagine stepping back into your body, sitting in the movie theatre. Through those eyes notice the screen is paused at the end of the movie. Press the rewind button and watch as the movie plays backward from safe point to safe point, and from the end to the start.

Once you reach the start, press the fast forward button, and watch as the movie speeds forward through all the steps of your wedding and reception until once again it reaches the end.

Repeat this process many times. Rewinding the movie. Then fast-forwarding it. Watching it spin back to the start, and then speeding through from beginning to end at the fastest playback speed.

You should notice a significant lessening of your emotional anxieties about being watched, speaking your vows, or being the center of attention. Your fears may disappear altogether.

The One & Only

There's strength in numbers. With this meditation, I want you to imagine cloning yourself. There are two ways you can do this.

1. Put your face on everyone else

You may be frightened of other people, but you aren't scared of yourself. Therefore, mentally photoshop your face onto those of your wedding officials, your fiancé, bridesmaids, friends, family, guests, vendors, and service personnel. You can even plaster your visage on inanimate objects like The mystics, sages and gurus say we are all One. This is a great way to get a sense of that. If there's only 'you' out there, there's nothing to fear!

2. Surround yourself with cloned doubles

In this version, you can leave everyone else as they are, but imagine you are surrounded by additional facsimiles of yourself. How many do you need to feel strong and confident in the face of all your guests? Start with one extra you at your shoulder, then add another on the other side. Picture three identical versions of you, in identical wedding dresses, all with one mind. Need more? No problem. Add more clones to be your allies until you feel well supported. There's an army of you now! On the one hand, they give you a feeling of support and strength in numbers, on the other, you can 'hide' amongst all these versions of you because the attention will be shared across them. When you're 'at the altar' just imagine these additional versions of yourself all around you backing you up 100%!

Do The Twist

In this mini-meditation – which you can pretty much do anywhere and on the fly – you are going to go from being a wedding worrier to an eco-warrior!

Environmentalists are all about recycling, right? We are going to take your biggest wedding waste product – your fears and anxieties – and recycle them. We'll give those negative energies a whole new positive purpose and drive. Sound good?

Let's say you've got a bit of glossophobia. The mere thought of speaking your vows or making a speech in front of your groom, friends, family, and guests, makes you break out in a sweat. Can you hear that little negative mantra playing over in your mind? "I'm scared, I'm frightened, I'm nervous!" it whines.

Let those labels fall to the floor for a moment. Just go inside and feel the energy sensation without putting a label on it.

Maybe you feel a sort of surging in your stomach? A tingling in your hands? Your heart beating faster? You've been calling it 'fear,' but you can recycle it by calling it 'excitement' instead. When you are excited, you can feel a surging in your stomach, tingling in your hands, and a racing heart too, right?

Do the old switcheroo whenever you think 'fear'. Immediately put a positive spin on it and reinterpret it as 'excitement'!

Excitement gives you energy and makes things fun. Bring your excitement to the parts of your wedding that used to give you fear! Why be 'frightened' of giving a speech or being in the spotlight when you can be 'cxcited'?

Meditation 17:

From Bridezilla to Bride Thriller

Uh-oh...

We don't know how it happened, but somewhere along the line in the wedding planning process, you've turned into...

> "Bridezilla: Queen of the Marriage Monsters!"

Maybe you sampled some radioactive wedding cake while trawling for bakers or something?!

Who knows!

What we do know – *and by 'we', I mean your poor fiancé, family, friends, and vendors* – is that you've turned into a prize beeyatch!

Melting ears with your atomic breath and *"Skreeeonk"* roars of complaint is hardly becoming.

One glance of those red, pulsing, eye beams of fury dissolves the will-to-live of any supplier who can't offer exactly what you want.

As you stalk about, tail thrashing with irritation, would-be supporters scatter in alarm, fleeing those snapping T-rex jaws and electric bite!

I know you don't want your fiancé to start to worry he's getting hitched to a hag from hell, so...

...This wedding reign of terror has got to stop!

Take a swig from the meditation antidotes below to un-hulk you from your full-on bridal sulk. You'll soon switch back from bridal beast to happily betrothed beauty once more.

Decompress, Dear

We all get it. Organizing a wedding is a mammoth task. But you mustn't let it turn you into a big angry woolly mammoth!

So, prepare yourself for meditation with either of the progressive relaxation, following the breath, box breathing, or 100-to-0 backward count methods listed at the start of this book.

Ready?

Deflate the Balloon of Fury

Feel all the tension, stress, and rage that's built up inside you about organizing *"this $%&**^$ wedding!"*

Now turn it up.

Yes, you heard me right. Make those horrible feelings even stronger. Turn that dial to the red zone. Feel the pressure stretching your seams to bursting point. Hear the hot hiss of fury, that sense of being completely overwhelmed.

Imagine you are like an overfilled balloon! You just want to scream and scream!

...

...

...

But, now, just untie the valve. Open it up and release the pressure.

Let it all go.

Let all that hot air and nonsense escape.

Imagine yourself flying around the room making a big wet farty noise as all that pressure whooshes out of you!

Finally, you land back on the ground with a flip-flap-flop. Emptied. Relaxed. You are freed of that burden.

Ahhhhhh... <let the sigh naturally come out of you>.

You Let The Dogs Out

Here's a second meditation to unleash your need to be a beast.

Imagine your inner bridezilla control freak as a great slathering hound growling and barking and attempting to bite anyone who comes near you.

This energy has got locked up inside you, where it has festered and chewed over its perceived bones of contention. It's a caged beast that keeps getting cattle-prodded by your stress. No wonder it is red-eyed and furious.

You need to let it go. That doesn't mean unleashing its meanness on others. It simply means to set it free so that it can stop barking and ruining the experience of planning your big day.

So, feel all that snarling tension within.

Notice where it is within you. Then simply imagine opening a door in front of it.

Imagine that dark energy 'dog' running out of you, running off into fields or into the sky. Notice it shrinking, turning into a harmless and playful puppy, as it runs away into the distance taking all that hurt, and pain, and stress away with it.

Welcome To Be Free

What you resist persists. Therefore, in this third melt-your-monster meditation, I want you to welcome that tension, stress, and sense of being overwhelmed that you feel burning inside you when in full-on Bridezilla mode.

You want to push it away, of course. To deny it or ignore it. You want to repress it because you don't want to acknowledge those feelings. You don't want to see yourself as a bitch or be thought of as a crazy bitch by anyone else. But that repression, that resistance, merely keeps the feeling stuck inside you.

Hale Dwoskin of the Sedona Method says to welcome those feelings as best as you can.

That means to be kind towards them. To notice them and allow them to be. Give them space to exist in your consciousness without trying to suppress or resist them. Just feel the feeling without labeling it as good or bad, positive or negative.

If you have practiced loving from your heart center, you can direct some love at those feelings.

How about that? Radiating loving energy at those inner 'beeyatch' feelings!

After you've done that for a while, you may notice the intensity of the feelings lessens.

Thinking of this inner feeling, you can then ask yourself, "Could I let this go?"

And, of course, you *could* let it go. It is entirely *possible* to let it go. Because it is just a feeling associated with a thought. And You are the boss of your mind.

So, answer Yes to that one.

Then ask yourself, "Would I be willing to let it go?"

Do you want to be free? Do you want your peace of mind back?

If so, the answer, again, has to be Yes.

Feel inside for that confirmation.

Last, ask yourself, "When?"

Right now would be a great time to let it go! So, when you get that "Now!" answer within your mind, just imagine letting go of those feelings that you first welcomed and are now setting free.

Emotion is meant to be in motion, meaning it comes into your consciousness and is then meant to pass out of you again.

When you resist it, you stop it, and it gets trapped within you where it just emotes without moving on.

Learn to let it go so you can live in freedom and joy!

To further explore the practices of releasing, going free and developing imperturbability, check out the teachings of the late Lester Levenson, taught via The

Sedona Method (Hale Dwoskin), or The Release Technique (Larry Crane), or The Power of Quiet (Kris Dillard).

MEDITATION 18:

OUT-OF-THIS-WORLD WEDDING

Whether your wedding is to be a small and intimate affair or vast and packed with guests, you have a LOT invested in trying to make it perfect!

Of course, the bigger the wedding, the greater the potential for things to go wrong. However, as stress is primarily generated internally, whatever its scale and however complex or simple your wedding is planned to be, you could find yourself turning into a bit of a lunatic while trying to put it together.

Which makes *this* the ideal meditation for you...

Houston We Have A Problem

When even thinking about your wedding plans stresses you out, take that inner fire burning in your stomach as a signal to launch yourself into a deep, peaceful space.

Get yourself ready for meditation, and then begin a NASA-style rocket launch countdown.

Imagine yourself in the capsule of a space shuttle on the launch pad at the Kennedy Space Center in Florida. The count starts, and you feel the tension building with each count.

"1 – 2 – 3 – 4 – 5 – 6 – 7 – 8 – 9 – 10 and we have lift off!"

Imagine you hurtle up from planet Earth out beyond the atmosphere and into deep space, leaving all your problems and worries behind.

Smoothly and easily fast-forward towards the Moon and then decelerate and make a perfect landing upon its surface.

A door lowers to form a ramp, and you step out on to the dusty pebble-strewn surface.

Swoon Walk

If you are into realism, you can wear a space suit and astronaut helmet… otherwise, glam up and look the business for your outing on the lunar landscape.

You'll notice that that dear pioneering man, the late Neil Armstrong, not only took one giant leap for mankind but, with remarkable foresight, left a beautiful swing seat for you to sit on and look back at the 'blue pearl' of Planet Earth!

Take your seat on the cushions, get comfortable, and relax.

You are 384,400 km away from your wedding and all the pressing things that seemed so important and worrying when they were right up in your face.

Finally, you have some perspective.

Imagine holding your hand up, making a hoop with your index finger and thumb, and gazing at the Earth which fits in the hoop of your fingers.

All those teeny tiny people down there!

Look at the vastness of the Universe around you. That wedding of yours, that threatened to overwhelm you, it doesn't seem so scary now, does it?

You can calmly think through the things you still need to do or organize. Contemplate the various aspects of your nuptials from this peaceful vantage point. Deep in the silence of outer space – the outer space in your inner space.

Let this distance and space seep into your mind like a balm of cool, calm, collectedness.

Allow this vast perspective to heal your mind, soothe away your stresses, and evaporate your concerns.

Know, at the core of your being, that you can handle anything that life throws your way.

Be a Lifelong Loony!

Take a relaxing Meditation Moon Shot whenever you need to regain perspective on life and get a big picture overview...

Meditation 19:

SHE'S SO SERENE

There's something so wonderfully pure about the sight of a bride in her white wedding dress. In all the best wedding fantasies you've ever seen visualized, whether in movies or in the theatre of your imagination, she moves with a magical tranquillity and grace that is totally captivating.

Wouldn't YOU like to be *that* kind of bride? Comporting yourself with both dignity and composure?

Even if you are a total scatterbrain, wild cat, or Calamity Jane most days, I'm sure you'd like to present yourself in the very best light at this most auspicious of times: Your union with your beloved.

To that end, let's meditate…

Swanning Around

1. Use one of your favorite methods to enter meditation.

2. In this meditation on developing serenity and gracefulness, we will adopt the imagery of a beautiful swan. You can picture one now, on a lake, canal, river, or castle moat, gliding silently over the water's surface, causing barely a ripple as it passes by.

The swan is a most apt symbol to choose for your wedding, not least because swans are said to mate for life.

3. Imagine that you will metamorphose into a beautiful swan on the day of your wedding so that you can move just as smoothly and as sleekly, without ruffling so much as a single feather.

4. In mythology, this ability to shapeshift and take on the form of an animal is known as *therianthropy*. The beautiful angel-like Valkyries of Norse myths would disguise themselves as swans when weighing the worthiness of men to enter Valhalla.

Swan Maiden: In various tales, these mythical 'swan maidens' would discard their swan skin disguises when they needed to bathe in a woodland spring or brook. A man would then chance upon her, falling instantly in love or lust. Our rather non-PC 'hero' would then hide her swan skin, so that she could not fly or swim away, and make her his wife!

5. In your mind's eye, imagine the journey you will take from your accommodation to your wedding venue, the entryway to the venue, and the aisle if your wedding features one, along which you will pass through your guests to meet up with your fiancé and the wedding officiant.

6. Envisage a path of golden light along this route from your start point through all the steps you will take on your wedding day. This loving path of light reaches a depth just below your navel and is perfectly smooth and radiant on its mirror-like surface. You will float along this pathway, buoyed and supported by this loving energy flow.

7. Now, picture this: You are dressed in your wedding outfit, your hair and make-up is perfect, and you are

moments from departing for the place where you will wed.

Just imagine that you close your eyes, inhale slowly and deeply, and begin the transformation process.

Whether you will be wearing a white dress or not, you can imagine giant white angel-like wings sprouting from your back, your neck lengthening, the lines of your body becoming sleeker, smoother and even more elegant. Perhaps your eyes glow with new depth, taking on that slightly demure cast that I think Audrey Hepburn often embodied so well in her movies.

Calling all swannabes: Do you really need to change from a human into a swan in this meditation? Not necessarily. You can play it that way the first time to get a deeper feeling of *'swanness'*. Otherwise, simply imagine it as a swan-like spiritual presence that 'overlays' your human form with a glowing radiance. This overlay can saturate you with the feeling of being swanlike – able to move through life with that peaceful grace and serenity.

Meditation 20:

Planning for Joy

You are going to get married, so why not decide right now to enjoy every moment of it?

More than that. Choose to find JOY in every moment of your engagement and every aspect of the lead-up to your wedding. Wouldn't that be great?

Many people find it hard to truly enjoy themselves. They struggle to hit the heights of joy. Some feel they don't deserve it. Some don't know how to let go enough to be able to feel it.

Some fear what others will think of them if they go around in a perma-state of happiness. Or get superstitious and nervous that something bad will happen to topple their 'excessive' glee.

Others live in their intellect and strangle their emotional life. We're all guilty at times of over-thinking and letting our thoughts spoil or limit the potential richness of our experiences, that's for sure.

Yet the romance of a loving betrothal is and always has been made for Joy.

To be reminded of that, Jane Austen fans need only think of the giddy happiness of Eliza Bennet and her beloved sister, Jane, when they receive and accept their proposals from Mr Darcy and Mr Bingley.

Romance, in both print and film, has always celebrated the sublime delight of the successful culmination of a courtship.

Surely you deserve that too?

Let's get to it, first by increasing your tolerance for joy.

The title of a best-selling book asked, 'How Much Joy Can You Stand?'.

We're about to shift your answer along the spectrum that runs from *none* -- to *a little* -- to *some* -- to *a lot* -- to *"Bring it on! I'm ready for bliss!"*

Increase Your Capacity

Having readied yourself for meditation, I want you to imagine that inside you is a special dial that controls your capacity for feeling elated. Please don't over-think this. Just assume it is there and whatever kind of Joy Capacity Dial you are imagining now, take that and use it.

Let's suppose that your capacity dial is turned to a lowish setting. Simply reach into this internal space of your being, grab hold of the dial, and turn the pointer to the maximum setting. You can imagine feeling a giant capacious space opening up within you. This gives you the room and tolerance space to feel super expanded levels of Joy.

Juice Up The Jouissance

Notice that next to your Joy Capacity Dial, there are three sliders. The first is labeled Gratitude. The Second is labeled Joy. The third is labeled Bliss. They are all set to base or normal levels. But you can reach out and, one by one, push the slider higher.

Start with gratitude: Push the gratitude slider up and notice that it lights up and glows with a vibrant dark pink color. Feel your sense of thankfulness and delighted gratitude bloom within you for your good fortune.

Move to Joy: Push the Joy slider higher and watch as it lights up and glows bright orangey-red. Feel your joy at getting married blossom and grow spreading smiles throughout every cell of your being. You feel so blessed!

Next is Bliss: Push the bliss slider up and observe how the slider lights up with a yellow color that becomes luminous gold at its peak. Simultaneously allow yourself to breath deeper and be bowled over with growing feelings of euphoria and bliss. Saturate in bliss!

(You can always add additional sliders to increase the intensity even more if you feel it's needed.)

Renew and Rejoice

Habituation to pleasure can cause some brides to lose sight of their happiness. It doesn't matter what your pleasure – chocolate, sex, shopping, kittens – if you eat it, do it, or stroke it without pause or end, eventually it stops registering as fun!

That's why the gratitude slider is so valuable. To evoke and feel gratitude, it's natural to refer back and forth from not having a thing to having it. From the pain, loneliness, or hunger of not having it, to the pleasure, love, and fulfillment of having it.

Don't be afraid to practice what the Stoics call 'negative visualization' to re-stimulate your jouissance juices.

Thinking back to when you were single and lonely and desperate for love before you met your fiancé, can renew your feelings of joy. Similarly, imagining what your life would be like if they suddenly died, left you, or had never been in your life, can remind you of all the reasons you have to rejoice that they are in your life today.

In your meditation, take yourself to the dark place, where death will inevitably come to take us all. We don't know where or when.

The recognition and acknowledgment that everyone you love, including your spouse-to-be, is here by the grace of Life, and could depart at any time, is a heavy thing to bear; but it will help you more fully appreciate the life you have, right now, with them still very much in it with you.

The Bag of Sweet Delights

Speaking of habituation, there is no need to habituate to the word Joy. In this meditation, I want you to imagine that you are sitting on a bench with your beloved beneath a tree in a beautiful garden on a lovely summer's day.

You both haven't a care in the world. You only have eyes for each other. You are so happy. Between you is a paper bag full of candies. These are special 'Love Hearts' candies which feature a heart on one side of the sweet with a word in it.

The words include Joy, Bliss, Delight, Ecstasy, Elation, Glee, Exultation, Gratification, Gratitude, Satisfaction, Wonder, Rapture, Rejoicing, Paradise, Heavenly, Exuberance, Jubilation, Love, Nirvana, and Euphoria.

Picture each of you taking turns to reach into the bag and pull out a candy. You read the word and then feed it to your partner or they feed it to you. Each of you is then overcome with that specific feeling as you suck, chew and enjoy the candy!

> *"To get the full value of joy, you must have someone to divide it with."*
>
> *~ Mark Twain*

Let the sweetness and the emotion the word describes mingle and saturate your experience.

The Permission Slip

If you ever find you struggle with allowing yourself to feel joy, just take a few moments in meditation and bring into the theatre of your mind the people that most inspire you. They can be alive, from history, or even legendary or spiritual figures of whom there is little concrete knowledge. It can be an authority figure or whatever represents the highest and best of life or your sense of what created you. It can be your higher self, your child self, or your soul. Whoever you choose will be perfect.

Bring this person, being or energy to mind, and visualize them giving you a beautiful piece of parchment. On this fine paper, in shimmering golden letters, it says:

"You <your name>, deserve to feel Joy, and you have my permission, and you have Life's permission to feel Joy now."

Let this be the key that unlocks your joy.

Repeat often to yourself, "I give myself permission to feel joy! Joy is good! I love my wonderful, joyous life!"

"Joy is what happens to us when we allow ourselves to recognize how good things really are."

~ Marianne Williamson

MEDITATION 21:

HAPPY EVER AFTER

There's the wedding. And then there's the *marriage*....

Ever wonder what the reality of living with your partner for the rest of your life (or the rest of his) is going to be like?

As if you haven't got enough concerns and worries about the wedding itself, many brides-to-be fret and drive themselves crazy about the future of their marriage before they've even wed!

"What if we run out of things to say to each other?"

"What if he stops making an effort and lets himself go?"

"What if we stop liking each other?"

"What if our jobs keep us apart, and we lose that special connection we have now?"

"What if we don't achieve our goals and end up struggling as so many people do?"

"What if my needs and wants change as I get older, and my husband won't get on board with those?"

"What if we fall out over money?"

"What if he cheats on me... or I am tempted to cheat on him?!"

...Yaddaa, yadda, yadda!

Fear feelings create fear thoughts which create more fear feelings which create more fear thoughts. *Ad nauseam.*

You've got to break the chains of negativity before they tie you to the very life outcomes you fear.

If you're willing to take charge of your destiny, you can create the fairy tale life of happiness and joy you want.

It's a matter of decision AND then follow-through.

First, decide upon the married life you want to have.

One full of joy, love, co-operation, shared adventure, friendship, fun, and laughter.

Then make an irrevocable decision within yourself that you will take responsibility for creating THAT life.

Moment by moment. Minute by minute. Day by day.

If you can have this conversation with your other half, and elicit a similar commitment, so much the better. Frame your marriage as a work of art that you will create together, constantly adjusting, improving, making more magical every day.

A great marriage is built by tiny actions that take place every day – even when you are bone-tired, in need of distraction, or pissed-off with the world and everyone in it!

Perhaps you will need some kind of framework of daily habits to help you stay true to your promise?

Like an unbreakable commitment to at say at least one "I love you!" every single day, deliver X-number of smoochy kisses and hugs per day no matter what, or like a good girl guide or scout, perform at least one or two acts of kindness for your beloved per day.

Don't forget the sexy stuff too. Intimacy is the bedrock of passion. The pleasure of touch will keep you connected. It's called 'love-making' for a reason. You'll want to keep making that love *strong* in your relationship.

Let's meditate on YOUR happy ever after.

Relax and get centered within yourself.

Imagine the highway of married life stretching out before you.

This is the path you will follow, hand-in-hand, as you travel into the Life that awaits ahead of you both.

When you embark on any long journey, you accept that you will pass through many different types of terrain. There will be obstacles and hold-ups along the way. There will be smooth open roads and freeways, and sometimes narrow, winding, pot-holed paths.

The marriage journey is no different. There will be ups and there will be downs. But as long as you have that commitment to loving one another through the thick and thin of life, of having each other's back, you will enjoy the heck out of it!

So, imagine that highway of your life stretching into the future. Feel into your heart for the love you hold for your partner. Project that love as a beam of light – a solid forcefield of grace – a wave of blessing power that rolls down that timeline highway, through all the months and years that you will share it.

Imagine it having a steamroller effect, smoothing out the worst bumps in the road. See it filling potholes and covering your path with the smoothest of surfaces. Every centimeter and every inch of the road is a moment in time of the life you will share. And that love is going forth ahead of you, 'pre-paving' the road, filling each of those moments and every part of your journey with grace, blessings, and the opportunity to thrive in happiness and joy.

You can touch down at any moment, imagining yourself in different scenarios – buying a new home, raising a family, changing careers, and dealing with occasional sickness, and in each instance, picture yourselves coping admirably as a couple.

Feel your bond ever strengthened by time and experience. Imagine yourselves reinventing your relationship at different ages, keeping the freshness in it, and always working as a winning team.

Hear the laughter that you share and the great conversations you have about life, and about progressing and developing as a couple and/or family.

Life will come at you with challenges as well. Grandparents will pass on, parents will age, there will be losses to cope with, and difficult decisions to make.

Visualize both of you having strong emotional resilience — the capacity to bounce back fast no matter what.

Get intimate with love, NOW, while you feel it so strongly. Play with it. Get to know it. I like to think of it how the ancient Yogis and sages used to describe it – as an infinite ocean of love that resides in the heart center in the middle of your chest.

It's important to think of real Love as an energy, like the sun, which shines in all directions on everybody no matter who they are or what they are like.

Begin to think of Love like that and you will start to understand it as something separate from and bigger than our usual idea of romantic love.

At the moment, you may feel that all your loving feeling is coming from and dependent upon your closeness with your fiancé. If you think about it coolly, that puts tremendous stress upon a relationship and upon you. It can make you needy, like an addict. You can become so addicted to that good feeling you have from being around him, that you lose your awareness of how to love yourself or feel love independent of another person.

What am I talking about?

Think back to that idea of an infinite ocean of love in your heart center. In spiritual traditions, the ultimate journey, the ultimate relationship is one that reunites you with God, the Source, or Infinite Being.

If you put your attention on that spot in the middle of your chest and start to breathe in and out of that area, by using your imagination, you can start to feel a sense of love, of lovingness, that radiates as warmth and sweetness.

To trigger those warm feelings, think of things that delight you – your lover, your family, your closest friends, puppies, flowers, nature, anything that brings a smile of pleasure and gratitude as you think of it. Let it be as love. Feel it. Smile into it.

You can allow that loving feeling to be for you, breathing it in and delighting in it, directing it towards yourself. And you can allow it to radiate outwards (on your out breath) as a loving warmth, radiance and blessing to, first, those people, animals, places and things you care for and like, and, secondly, to the extended world beyond, including perhaps even those people you don't usually like or care for! You get extra good karma points for that!

This is tremendously liberating and empowering to discover that LOVE exists within you and can be tapped at any time.

It means you can 'refill your own pot', so to speak, without depending on another to do it for you. That doesn't mean you can't delight in the joy of intimacy and togetherness that a wonderful love marriage can bring. It just means that you are always in a position to be a strong and loving and happy person.

> "Let there be spaces in your togetherness, and let the winds of the heavens dance between you. Love one another but make not a bond of love: Let it rather be a moving sea between the shores of your souls. Fill each other's cup but drink not from one cup. Give one another of your bread but eat not from the same loaf. Sing and dance together and be joyous, but let each one of you be alone, even as the strings of a lute are alone though they quiver with the same music. Give your hearts, but not into each other's keeping. For only the hand of Life can contain your hearts. And stand together, yet not too near together: For the pillars of the temple stand apart, And the oak tree and the cypress grow not in each other's shadow."

~ Khalil Gibran, The Prophet

As you practice being the Source of Love or having the Source within you, that can have a tremendous effect on your spiritual life, giving your life much deeper meaning.

For those who define themselves as atheists, the practice can be experienced as simply a wonderful way to develop emotional resilience and good mental health. Think of it as 'well-being,' a deep well and reservoir of loving beingness within you.

By tapping into this love, you can direct it into your life, you can aim it at those who need it, and you can always draw upon it to be loving. This will prove useful in stressful times when, let's say, your normal romantic feelings towards your partner are clouded over by the circumstances.

This is about becoming conscious in your relationship and honoring your commitment to love the other... no matter what.

With this power, you will ride through any storm and emerge triumphant as a couple.

It's very easy to be dependent. To look to others to rescue you or make you feel good. To live with real power, however, means to take responsibility for your life and exercise your creativity to make the best of life.

Tap the love. Be the love. And enjoy a wonderful married life. You can do it!

In closing, I offer this blessing to you and your beloved...

May your hearts be always full of Love.

May you always appreciate one another and thank Life with all your being for placing you together.

May you grow rich in gratitude and the well-being of living joyfully, purposefully, and productively together.

May your flourish and thrive as a couple and be an inspiration for others to love as wisely and abundantly as you do.

May you have the best of fun, fill your lives with laughter, and relish every precious moment!

May all blessings abound upon you!

I love you!

Author's Note

Thank you for purchasing and reading this book. I trust that you have enjoyed and had fun experimenting with the meditations.

Hopefully, they have brought you some peace of mind and will help smooth your journey from being a Miss to a Mrs!

I think the key to life is to take an experimental attitude, bring your full creativity and sense of humor to bear on the challenges we all face, think BIG and really embrace the power of your mind.

Go do wonderful things!

Will you help me?

If you enjoyed this book, please take a few moments to leave a positive review on Amazon, letting others know what you liked about it. And recommend it to your friends too!

Thank you so much.

Wishing YOU abundant joy and boundless love in your marriage and throughout every part of your life,

Madison Bound

Printed in Great Britain
by Amazon